A Powerful New Data Tool for Real Estate Profes...

JACKED UP

The Rules Have Changed

Real Estate Data Secrets that Google and Brokerages
Do Not Want You to Know

EDDIE GODSHALK, MBA

FIRST PRINTING EDITION MMXX

Copyright © 2021 Eddie Godshalk

ISBN: 978-0-578-79321-4

Jacked Up: The Rules Have Changed
Real Estate Data Secrets That Google & Gurus Don't Want You to Know

Contact: Eddie Godshalk
Email address: info@zipanalyser.com
Website: www.zipanalyser.com
Phone number: 408-755-0071

CONTENTS

Testimonies:

'Jacked UP' describes how new technology is changing the way Real Estate professionals' access never before available market data. Now Realtors can position yourself as the local leader and authority. Learn how to make more profits and sales, while lowering risk, with new market DATA, local forecasts, and APIs.

Marie Antonette G. Waite, Founder and CEO
Finest Women in Real Estate / Fire-Up Connect

"Data and Information is the currency to success and wealth in real estate. Without it you're operating in the dark without a compass. 'Jacked Up' shows you how to use data to navigate real estate as a buyer or investor."

Marco Santarelli, Founder & CEO,
Norada Real Estate Investments

"Data is the equivalent to digital oil in today's digital revolution. For the first time in history technology enables real estate professionals to do as much business in as many places as we want to. The only question is where do you drill? This book provides a roadmap into the world of real estate data and will make you a smarter and more advanced real estate professional for reading it, giving you a competitive advantage over your peers. "

Andreas Senie, RE Tech Thought Leader
Founder & CEO CRE Collaborative Inc
Founder & Partner EAC Properties LLC

My Origin Story

How I got Here and Why it Matters to You.

I was sitting 40 stories up in the air, sitting on cold steel in -10° weather. My ZZ-Top beard and my fu-man-chew mustache were a solid cube of ice, because of the howling wind and my running nose. I looked down at my motorcycle, just a back dot in the snow, and knew that I could not do this much longer; besides, I was in one of the most dangerous professions there was. Walking on slick steel in the snow made ironworking seemed too unbearable for much longer. When I got home, I bitched and bitched to my older brother, while he just listened. As I completed my bitching session, my brother said, "You know, Eddie, anybody can complain."

I took it to heart and decided to **DO something**. I read every book on wealth, business, and real estate available. I studied every real estate guru training book, and tapes. Yes, there were tapes back then, so you can guess how old I was.

Over the next eight years, I made hundreds of offers, talked with thousands of brokers, bought over one-hundred properties, six of them being no money down. I flipped some and exchanged others to increase my cash and cash flow. I accumulated over $4 million in real estate and had over 20 single-family and four small apartment buildings. I had it made, or so I thought. But - **something unexpected happened.**

The Savings & Loan Crisis hit, and prices declined over 50%. During this time, a settlement attorney also bounced a large settlement check. I went from "retired" and living in a 4,000 square foot home in a nice area of Washington D.C. to living in my car. After many months of emotional devastation, I was either going to die in my car, or change. Again, I decided to **DO something** and drove to California, where my discovery journey began. I wanted to know what I could have done differently. What did I do wrong? None of the realtors, brokers, trainers, or books had any information on when to sell!

I eventually got my MBA with a focus on building Automated Valuation Models (AVMs) as my graduate thesis. However, just knowing the Present Value (PV) did not help me much, or accurately assess real estate ownership risk. So, I got a "job" in banking with a portfolio lender. While working with the Quality Control (QC) and risk departments. I found out about monthly and quarterly economic and demographic data. The QC department monitored monthly and quarterly growth in median income and other economic data, at all Zip Codes and submarket levels. The bank used this growth data to help determine if the bank would keep or sell their loans.

The bank bought and aggregated (compiled) the same data that big retailers like Starbucks, Target, and big builders like Toll Brothers use to determine where to build, and where to locate new stores. I asked my PhD friends at Berkeley and UCLA if this data could be used to build predictive models. I got a "maybe" as a response.

Still, it is imperative to note, that none of the data we buy, and aggregate is free or "pullable," so most people and businesses are not aware that the data even exists. As stated, only the big retailers and builders are aware, because they have serious money at risk in making their location decisions. Then began another 5+ year journey of data aggregation and testing until we finally built the predictive models that we have today. The forecasting models we have built are the most accurate in the real estate industry.

Currently, many of our subscribers know what is going on more than any other Realtor or investor. But then something happened in 2020. No, it was not a virus; it was a connection on LinkedIn that found me. He said, "Eddie, this data and technology is amazing, but no one knows about it or you. So, why don't you build some APIs so that I and everyone can access the data?"

Then the light when on. It had always been my passion, not to make money, and not to build software, but to democratize the core missing data that is missing in the industry. Moreover, the best way to get this data out to everyone is through APIs and widgets.

An application programming interface or API is a computing interface and set of programming code which defines interactions between multiple software intermediaries. Although an APIs is not a common term to most consumers, according to Postman, every piece of software built today either uses an API, or is an API.

Now, the only real issue is how do we educate the industry that this data exists? This is the reason for my new book.

It is hard to know where to buy and when to sell. No one knows since the data needed to make these decisions are not available from a Google search, website, or any app. The data is not on the web. You might think that using old information is alright for real estate. However, if you do not know EXACTLY where to buy, EXACTLY when to buy, and EXACTLY when to sell properly, you will not be successful in real estate. You may get LUCKY, but smart real estate decisions must be DATA-DRIVEN, not Hope-Driven, for long-term success.

If you disagree, you probably should not read my book, or use our APIs, or current market data. It is not for you. Return it and get a refund. In the movie "The Matrix," Neo has a choice to take the Red Pill or the Blue Pill.

These are the only two choices.

Morpheus explains that Neo is a slave to the world as he takes the Blue Pill. Things will go back to the ways he wants to believe. But if Neo takes the Red Pill, his eyes will be opened, and the truth will set him free.

The same can be said as you choose between being "Data-Driven" or "Opinion-Driven." The data-driven person can make decisions based upon facts and data, while the opinion-driven, stays in the current system of the world, which is full of confusion and distrust. Ultimately, this is your choice, just like in "The Matrix."

If you pick the Blue Pill, stop reading altogether.

Ultimately, we believe all real estate professionals have the right to have access to the most current submarket growth data, leading economic indicators, and accurate submarket forecasts, to make smarter buying and selling decisions.

Today, real estate professionals and investors are flying blind since such data does not exist online. It is from this struggle that we have built Zip Analyser.

Zip Analyser comes with real-time data visualization and new APIs and dashboards. With our data visualization technology search across over 310,000 U.S. markets, and never leave your office - a significant time and money saver. Also, filter and add custom weights to leading economic indicators. Discover the right locations for your investments or business in a snap.

With our new APIs, you now can choose the Red Pill.

Which do you choose?

Introduction and How to Use the book

The "X" You Cannot Afford to Miss

For those of you who choose to take the Red Pill and openminded enough to grow and evolve, keep going, since change is just a fact of life. For those who are at least willing to consider taking the Red Pill, here is some background, and how to use this book. First get educated, get smart, and then you can make more profits, no matter what aspect or sector within the real estate industry you are in. In nearly all aspects, data has an effect. The choice is yours and begins with getting educated.

We evolved from a group of residential and commercial real estate investors, developers and real estate professionals who have experienced first-hand the herculean effort, and months it takes to find a deal. We are keenly aware of the huge risk of holding real estate short and long-term. Especially with no clue or knowledge of when the next decline will occur, or where to reinvest.

For the past four plus years we have been developing break-through solutions based upon the aggregation of crucial data at the market and submarket levels. Data that is not easily accessible or found on the web today.

We wanted to make this data accessible and easy to use, so we have developed a system to express its output in easy to understand heatmaps and new API graphs. With new APIs and new technology real estate professionals and real estate investors will finally have the power OF data, to adequately assess local submarket risk, and opportunities, to make more profits and commissions.

Our Mission:

We believe all real estate professionals have the right to access the most current market and submarket growth data, economic indicators, and submarket forecasts, to make informed buying and selling decisions. And with the power of data access, lower your risk while, at the same time, make smarter real estate decisions. Today real estate professionals and investors are flying blind Because such data does not exist online. It from this struggle, we built Zip Analyser.

That is why we built Zip Analyser – you will learn:

- The "X" you cannot afford to miss.

- Learn about why no one has fixed the fundamental problems of data access.

- Learn about and new data-driven solutions with new APIs, dashboards, and customizable real-time data visualization technology.

- Learn how to find the right locations for your investments or business, in a snap.

- Discover new data and interactive images to add to your reports and websites to gain the power of current local market data and local expertise.

CHAPTER 1

Myths and Misconceptions

Five major myths and misconceptions that can cause you major financial and opportunity loss.

Before we start discussing why real estate is Jacked UP, first, we need to discuss some core myths and misconceptions within the entire US real estate industry.   You need to know this first and be aware.   Because these myths and misconceptions are the core causes of risk and financial loss.

MYTH #1

Myth: When assessing risk, opportunities, and making more profits/sales/commissions, real estate professionals have access to the most current market data and submarket data.

Myth #1 – Is the **BIGGEST** myth and misconception across the **ENTIRE** real estate industry.

Real estate professionals and real estate investors have access to public and low-cost datasets. But little to no access to any current leading economic indicators, such as the latest growth in population, income, or new jobs, as explained in greater detail in Chapter 11. It is pretty surprising when you think about it, since real estate, is the largest investment many people make.

It is **NOT** true that once an agent is licensed, they have access to all the current local data needed to advise an investor, homebuyer, or seller. Most real estate training only teaches extremely basic facts. Like how not to get sued. Most agents do NOT have access to the current market data or submarket data. They focus primarily on property data. The lack of data is one reason why, according to Gallop Polls, over 67% of all Americans do not trust real estate professionals.

It is **NOT** true that within their MLS (Multiple Listing Service) licensed real estate professionals have an easy way to advise their clients which markets or submarkets to build and invest in. As well as, what other out-of-state submarkets, offer higher opportunities and returns. If anyone thinks this is true, just ask a real estate professional this simple question:

Ask This Simple Question:

What are the top Blocks and Tracts to invest in, in my city and why?

A Venture Capitalists (VC) Story

I remember it as though it were yesterday when I was at a VC pitch training here in Silicon Valley, and I wanted to get some feedback from the trainer. He asked if anyone would like to practice a 60-second pitch. I fervently started waving my hand and gave my 60-second pitch about the fundamental problems within real estate, and the core missing data.

He responded in confusion, I guess because we have such disruptive data **AND** technology. He asked me to give an example of the data I was talking about. So, I said, for example, "What is the latest population growth based upon February 2021 data in the Zip Code we are in, in Zip Code 95125." He smiled and whipped out his iPhone and pressed a few tabs and said, "Hey

Google, what is the latest population growth in Zip Code 95125 in San Jose, California." And Google "spoke" back and we all could hear Google say, "the Population in Zip Code 95125 is 52,729." He pointed his phone at me and said – "Here is the answer. Google says it is 52,729."

I asked him when this data was last updated. He said, "Google does not say." I pointed out to him that this is a stale useless static number, not a growth number. He then said, "But that is **ALL** that Google says."

I explained to him that this was an old stale data number, and NOT a growth data number. I told him the answer should be a percentage number because, it is a percent growth in population, a key factor that influences local real estate prices and risk. He replied. But this is what "Google says."

I knew then, I had a major educational challenge

I have been with more than my fair share of myopic Luddites before, so I knew I was in for a challenge. I knew at that moment that I had a challenge on my hands. Since it is **NOT** that Google is lying, or that Realtors, or websites are "lying," it is that the data is not online. The Google AI search is just making its best guess.

However, the answer was and is **100% FALSE** and INACCURATE. Google AI does not answer the question because the answers are NOT online or even searchable.

Talking to Commercial Real Estate Brokers

I remember talking with a top Commercial Real Estate (CRE) broker years ago. I wanted to ask for his advice on my old website and software. We met in his office library. I explained to him about our current demographic and economic data, that is so critical in evaluating where to invest, and when to sell.

After 50 minutes of discussion, he finally got it, and understood. I made sure of it and made him repeat it back. He repeated back the core premise, that current local market data matters and why. It matters in CRE purchase making decisions. He acknowledged that the growth in new jobs, median incomes, and population growth, has a huge influence on land prices in both the residential and commercial real estate industries.

Then he said, "But there is a problem…."

He pulled two of his thick 700 plus page CRE textbooks off the shelf, and said – "Eddie, look at these." I chuckled inside because I suspected they would not have much on local market analysis or local risk assessment.

At that time, some of my best friends and contacts had PhDs from UC Berkeley and UCLA. My PhD friends clearly understood that even the top PhDs in Real Estate, Macroeconomics, and Microeconomics do not have access to local data, local growth data, or current submarket data – The **DRIVERS of RISK**. Because like the agents and brokers, the universities have NO access to current economic or demographic data. They ONLY have access to free or very low-cost yearly data.

Even the top PhD's at the top universities have no data access to the drivers of growth, local risk, or local economics. I looked at the textbooks that the CRE (Commercial Real Estate) broker handed me and began my discovery.

I flipped through the introduction, the table of contents, skimmed the back cover, and did not see much. So, I searched the Index in the back and searched for the following:

"Current market data" – and found **NOTHING**

"Current demographic data" – and found **NOTHING**

"Current economic data" – and found **NOTHING**

"Current market trends" – and found **NOTHING**

"Current market risk"– and found **NOTHING**

Then removed the word "current" and again, searched and found **NOTHING**. So, then I searched for:

"Leading Economic Indicators" – and found **NOTHING**

"Leading Demographic Indicators" – and found **NOTHING**

"Economic Risk Factors" – and found **NOTHING**

"Submarket Risk" – and found **NOTHING**

"Population Growth" – and found **NOTHING**

I did find one page in the Index pages, for "economics" but this was only for analysis on the property itself, **NOT** the market or submarket. Not the drivers of future CRE prices and risk, which are the changes in local economic factors. I kept searching and found the indexed word "demographics." Then looked at this indexed page and found two paragraphs of generic and vague text.

Guess what, I looked at three other textbooks and found the SAME thing.

This is fundamentally why no PhD in Real Estate or Economics knows about current market data. The data is not free, published, or "pullable." However, nearly every large builder and retailer knows about the data. They make their location-based decisions based on current data and current growth data. They do **NOT** make large financial decisions based on the results of a Google search, advertising website, someone's opinion, or wishful thinking.

BIG players have access, smaller players do NOT

No Certified Commercial Investment Member, no residential broker, no Commercial Real Estate broker, no REIT, or local real estate investment club, or "guru" has access.   This is the fundamental problem within the real estate industry, and why real estate is opaque and Jacked UP.   The data and facts for smart decision-making are not online or easily accessible and Jacked UP.

Then my CRE broker concluded - Today, people and real estate professionals have three choices.

1. Hope – make decisions based upon opinion and no current market data…. Gut feelings.

2. Use stale yearly data and some expensive quarterly metro market data.

3. Embrace new technology and join our software that has no APIs yet.

However, today, with this book, we are introducing a new fourth choice.   A choice based upon the original dream I had, to get the critical missing data to the real estate industry and help my fellow agents, brokers, and real estate investors.   To get the data to YOUR business and website.   As you read and learn more, you will learn about the fourth option. The fourth option involves new APIs and new real estate technology.

But first, let's look at another myth, the myth regarding property features.

MYTH #2

When assessing risk, opportunities, and making more profits/sales/commissions, what matters most is property features. It is a myth that property features such as the number of bedrooms, bathrooms, property age, building quality, and the like, have more influence than current local market growth data.

When assessing risk, there are two main categories – time and proximity. Depending upon when and where the risk factors are, depends upon if the risk is "nice to know" or critical. For instance, it is nice to know that a large forest fire and virus is happening somewhere in the US this year. However, it is critical to know that the fire or virus is knocking on your door this week, or now. Time and proximity make a **BIG** difference.

The same is true for property data, compared to current market data. Property data and features are nice to know but have no real influence on risk or profits.

Current real estate technology to access risk and rates of return, rely on assumptions that are based on general trends of stale yearly historic data. They tend to place limited attention on the location and property features compared to critical local-level Block Group factors that influence real estate risk and future value changes.

What if?

What if as a real estate professional, you could?

What if you could help a client and provide these answers. The basic questions that a prospect has, or a client asks. What if? Would you make more commissions? Everyone we have talked to, who has seen our new data and technology, always answers YES. However, they immediately ask.... **But HOW**? How can they answer their client's questions fast and easy? These answers are Coming Soon, in the following chapters.

In the Radio ad for Realtors – Light the Way: 30-second ad, it states that "No matter where you live, where you live has never mattered more. For over 100 years, Realtors have brought LOCAL KNOWLEDGE and DEEP EXPERTISE, to helping people to find new places to dream, and thrive." www.nar.realtor/thats-who-we-r   Today, no licensed agent or broker has access to current economic, demographic, or local market growth data. Therefore, how can they have great deep _____? This language is not exactly right. With NO access to submarket growth or critical facts, this is almost like the propaganda News from parts of our country that thrive on misinformation and uninformed listeners.

Ask any experienced person who has read this book and understands the core points, just ASK. Ask specific and quantifiable local data-driven questions. Local knowledge of what markets and submarkets? What Block Groups?
Deep expertise in what?

Deep experience in property data, in sales data, in driving around, in stale yearly data? In what?

They are saying we should "trust" the "Local Realtor" since they know the local market and submarket. But do they?

Challenge Your Assumptions

Your assumptions are your windows on the world. Isaac Asimov said "Your assumptions are your windows on the world. Scrub them off every once in awhile, or the light won't come in." Without challenging your assumptions, you and the world will be left in the world of opinions and NOT data-driven.

We can play the blame game, let's get the lucky game, and the Opinion Dad game, OR we can learn from the mistakes that were made, and choose to correct them with data.

One of the biggest benefits is if and when the data GAP is filled, you can alert your clients about upcoming market trends, and therefore, make more commissions.

Knowledge is Power, but only if used, and if the data is current.

When new data and API technologies are made available, we can roll back time and speculate about all past real estate losses, that might have been greatly neutralized. More importantly, going forward in time, you will have the data to focus on the factors that affect risk, opportunities, profits, and sales at the market and submarket levels.

MYTH #3

Myth: When assessing risk, opportunities, and making more profits/sales/commissions, what matters is Metro and City data and NOT local and submarket data.

MYTH: When city or metro market data indicates that the area is doing well, it means that every Block, Tract, Zip Code, household, and individual are also doing well. When the metro market or city is known to be a great place to invest, based upon stale yearly data, it is a good strategy to buy and invest there. It is always a good strategy because there is a high correlation to the City and Metro Market data, to local submarket data and trends.

In Fact: Within any large market, there are **ALWAYS** good and bad local markets. Just because LA or New York City will go up over 20% in the next 36-months, does **NOT** mean that every Block, Tract, or property will follow the same pace. Some may go up to around 40%, some may go down (-40%) in value.

This is just the way real estate works. This is how all large sets of data work. No city is homogenous. No city or metro market has the same neighborhoods or local markets. They are ALWAYS differences in every city and metro market in the US, and in the world. Any city with a population of over 50,000 will ALWAYS have different submarket growth patterns.

NO city or metro market in the US is homogeneous

It is not true that what matters most is the metro market or city data. Because metro market growth trends are not what drives local real estate prices or risk. If any salespeople or advertiser uses metro market trends to sell you a specific property this is a **BIG Red Flag** – Buyer Beware!
Buyer Beware

Las Vegas, Phoenix, San Francisco, Miami, or Los Angeles all may be great cities to invest in, in different times in the past or future, but any large market will ALWAYS have good and bad local markets and submarkets. Each will have different risk factors and opportunities, depending upon the Block and Tract trends and local market analytics.

The Driving Around Myth

Myth: Some real estate investors and real estate professionals "think" that they can "drive-around" any neighborhood to find enough local information to make smart investments and buying decisions.

In Fact, what makes a smart investment choice is having access to the core data and variables that do and **WILL** affect price movements in the future. In real estate, these variables include -

population changes, income changes, local economic changes, and local demographic changes. None of these datasets CAN be viewed or quantified by "driving around."

The idea that any real estate professional can "drive around," and thus learn about any local market data, is a completely false concept. This idea has evolved because we as "hunter-gathers," think that what matters most, is what we can see in our immediate field of vision. Since what we can immediately see is what we gather, harvest, and of immediate possible danger.

However, in real estate, what matters is NOT in our field of vision. Think about it. How many times would you have to drive around a Block, Tract, Zip Code, or a 1,000-foot radius, to discover the latest economic or demographic growth patterns? Or how many times would a drone, have to fly over with X-ray vision to monitor weekly population changes, new permits, new job growth, and recent migration....... Driving around is a 100% silly concept that can only really benefit big oil companies, not the investor, or the data-driven real estate professional.

Some consumers, real estate investors, and salespeople may think that just knowing the metro market trends and real estate price forecasts are good enough and use services from companies like Core Logic or Local Market Monitor. If you think this is true, make sure you read the next chapter carefully, do your research, and fill in the data in the **Start Here First Table**.

It is a false assumption that just knowing metro market data and metro market forecasts are sufficient. This assumption can cause devastation to your portfolio and extreme risk. Within a typical large metro market that WILL go up 30% in the next 36-months, there will be winners and losers. In most cases, historically, many Block Groups will go down by 25% and some will go up by 25% in value in the same 36-month time-period.

Real estate is NOT homogenous - local data, and local growth RULES. Therefore, we always want to know the local market data and facts, because they matter so much. Many lost millions in declining markets because they had no access to the current market data or facts. With the right data and facts, this Jacked Up industry will evolve, and change to more clarity, and certainty with less risk.

MYTH #4

Myth: When assessing risk, opportunities, and making more profits/sales/commissions, current market data is not needed in my market, because yearly data is good enough.

You may think that it is good enough to only use stale yearly data, and that it is OK to just focus on your feelings and emotional observations and experience in driving-around neighborhoods, after all, lots of people used to say:

- Everybody knows that the world is flat.

- Everybody knows that the earth is the center of the universe.

- Everybody knows that man will never reach the moon.

- Everybody knows that real estate always goes up in value.

But what eventually changes any false belief?   Facts, data, and new technology.

It is more of a question of, do you want to be ahead of the game, a progressive early adopter, or do you want to be told by others, that in fact, the world is not flat?

Yesterday and a Berkeley broker

I remember as if it was yesterday, I was talking to a top real estate broker in Berkeley, CA while visiting some of my PhD friends at UC Berkeley. We started discussing how we were building a platform that delivers current economic and demographic data and accurate local forecasts at the Block Group level. After 20 minutes or so, he finally understood that he did not have access to current local market data, nor did his Multiple Listing Service, his MLS in Berkeley.

After over 20 minutes of discussion, he just blurted out... Current market data does NOT MATTER in "my market!" I was not too sure how to respond, so I replied semi-jokingly and said....

"So, if New Job Growth, Median Income Growth, Business Growth, and the Growth in Disposable Income does not MATTER in your market, then WHY the heck are you even selling real estate in THAT MARKET, in a market like that?"

He went silent and did not know how to reply. This concept was new to him. He was so used to selling real estate based upon emotions. It was a big challenge for him to change his thinking from selling based upon emotions and property features alone to data-driven selling based upon facts and data.

Sometimes brokers get defensive

Sometimes brokers get defensive and say that we are trying to replace the real estate agent and broker with new data and technology. The answer is 'NO'. If you have been reading and understanding anything here, you will come to know that that is not the case or our mission. We are just providing a tool that delivers critical missing market data. I will be quite happy if I stay as a Data-Driven Dad, and few people come to our website. We can stay in the background and just deliver the data via our APIs. Or widgets on your website, where you can mashup your listings. The point is to give buyers and sellers, and **ALL** real estate professionals the option to access more current market data.

The mismatch of data silos

Where is the data for October 2020 on income growth or population growth? These are the main drivers of risk and prices at the Block and Zip Code levels, so we want to access the current data and numbers.

If a new listing is just now on the market, in October 2020, and the ONLY market data available is from January 2019, this data is over **18 months OLD**. Just show me the property that matches, that is available in January 2019, NOT 18 months LATER! If you want me to buy something based upon Jan 2019 data, then show me that listing from that time-period. Show me the listing from January 2019 based upon the market data from January 2019! If you want me to buy a city or MSA, then show me the price of that. Just Crazy, the mismatch of silos of data and time-periods.

Some day in the future when real estate is no longer Jacked UP, and UN-Jacked, the data and technology will be available to everyone. It will be up to you if you want to stay myopic or not. At least we expect, sometime in 2021 you will have the option. The choice will be yours in 2021.

MYTH #5

Myth #5: When assessing risk, opportunities, and making more profits/sales/commissions, what matters most is appraised value, NOT local forecast value.

Homebuyers and investors often make their home purchase and property investment decisions based solely on appraisals and MLS-based information about housing prices. They assume that these sources provide accurate and reliable information that reflects the true market value of the property they intend to buy, and **ALL** relevant current local market information.

This myth affects the buyer's risk-reward decision. It is the reason why so many people go to the web to search for answers. It is a false assumption that what matters is the property value, while in reality the house or building does not change in value, the land changes in value. What affects land prices is typically not the house or building asset, but local variables and indicators. Local leading economic indicators are what matter the most, and have the biggest effect on risk and reward.

Most importantly, appraisals do not take into account **ANY** real estate growth data – the latest monthly updates, and factors such as the latest demographics changes, or economic supply and demand factors, or economic growth factors needed to make quantifiable predictions about future movements in prices at **ANY** local or geo-level.

Many real estate professionals use appraised value to get listings, and consumers use appraised value to view their perceived equity gains, which is OK and entertaining. However, this is not the best method or strategy to use if you are a buyer or seller, who wants to make a smarter fact-based decision, to make more profits, more sales, or commissions.

Appraised value also goes by many other names, such as market value, perceived value, index value, AVM (Automated Valuation Model) value, and present value. The appraised value is simply what an appraiser or some valuation system thinks that the asset is worth and will sell for that day. NOT what it will sell for in one month or in six months, but what it will sell for today.

Appraisal value systems use inputs or variables in their models, such as square footage, land square footage, comparable sales price, number of bedrooms, number of bathrooms, etc. Different property variables are adjusted to comparable sales, based upon their proximity to the subject appraised property. Comps are adjusted, and the appraised value is calculated.

Appraised value accuracy

In general, the accuracy of true appraisals, which are the ones that are done by licensed appraisers, are more accurate than any free or automated AVM. For instance, an entertainment and advertising site, Zillow, is known to be off by over ±10%; that is (plus or minus 10 percent) in some parts of the US. Where most licensed appraisals have an accuracy of ±2.5%; that is (plus or minus two-point-five percent).

Forecast value accuracy

Accurate forecast values are always based upon the "area." These areas and definitions are explained in greater detail in Chapter 4. It is just safe to say that the closer and more granular the forecast model is to the subject asset or property, the more valuable the forecasts are in making any data-driven real estate decision.

Forecast value systems or models use different inputs or variables as explained in greater detail in Chapter 12. Forecast models do NOT consider ANY property features, since these features ONLY have an influence on present values, not on future values. The different forecast models take into account different factors, such as sales price, repeat sales, aggregated sales price, sale price timing, current economics, current demographics, local growth factors, cluster analysis, and national factors such as interest rates and demand.

There are two types of forecasting models today. They each have a proven and back-tested accuracy of ±2.5%. The main difference in these two models are the inputs and outputs, because they take into account different variables and different data geo-coverage. One forecast model uses free property, sales, and title data, while the other uses non-public, or private off-line data such as the latest monthly updates of census block group median income growth.

One forecast model covers 7,000 US markets, while the other covers over 300,000 US markets. One helps the Data-Driven Dad, the other helps the Opinion Dad, as you will see in the next Chapters.

Today, there is a lot of misplaced focus in risk analysis based upon the appraised value, not local forecast value, because it is easy to do, and easier to automate. Appraisers charge hundreds of dollars for a new loan origination appraisal, depending upon the property type, appraisal type, and appraiser. But where is the real risk in just knowing the appraised value for the long-term owner of the asset? Or you?

Getting clearer - stocks for example

Let us take stocks for example when buying as a long-term investment. Which matters more, the price at purchase or the price of the stock in 36-months? The appraised value or local forecasts value? The price now, or the price in the future? Most data scientists and data-driven investors will agree that what matters is forecast value, right? Agree?

The EXACT same is true for real estate investing and ownership. However, real estate risk is in a fog of uncertainty for most real estate professionals. Because economic and demographic market data is updated **YEARLY**, NOT monthly, or quarterly in **ALL** submarkets, by ALL apps, search engines, and software today.

Risk managers, appraisers, loan originators, Realtors, real estate investors, and yes, even consumers, do NOT have access to current economic and demographic market data OR accurate local real estate forecasts. You cannot find the data, or answers by searching on Google, or even find the answers from subscription services.

What matters is NOT the current value of a stock or a real estate asset, UNLESS you are just flipping the asset to some other buyer or institution who is unaware of accurate local trends, growth, and accurate local real estate forecasts. What matters is local forecast values in nearly all cases when holding the ownership of the asset, PROVIDED that the predictive models are accurate at the local market level, at the Block, and Track levels.

To prove and illustrate that forecast value matters more than the present value, let us take a look at three scenarios. We are using Block Group or BG forecasts, because they are the smallest and most local boundary levels, where reliable data is updated every month or quarter. Thus, BGs are the "closest" to the property, and have the highest correlation to any property address in the US.

Below are three scenarios.

- Which property has the highest risk?
- Which property has the highest risk of potential loss?

#1: Property has an appraised value of $500,000 with an accuracy of ±2.5% - ($487,500 - $512,500).

#2: Property has a BG 36-month forecast value of +25% with an accuracy of ±2.5% - ($609,375 - $640,625).

#3: Property has a BG 36-month forecast value of **(-25%)** with an accuracy of ±2.5% - ($365,625 - $384,375).

In all three scenarios, the accuracy of both the present value and forecast value is the same, at ±2.5%.

Which of the 3 scenarios shows the highest risk and which would you buy?

Do you see a clear answer that is data-driven?

In #1 you are buying a property with the standard appraised value error of ±2.5%. Your risk is that you may be paying too much for the property. Diminish some risk by getting a second and third opinion and use free AVM services and check comparable sales.

In #2 you are buying a property with the standard Block Group (BG) forecast value error of ±2.5%. Your risk is minimal. However, your profit potential is exceedingly high.

In #3 you are buying a property with the standard BG forecast value error of ±2.5%. Your risk is EXTREME. Your potential loss of equity in 3 years is ($500,000 - $365,625) or (-$134,375).

The above is another example of decision making, using **DATA**. Surprisingly, some people still think that what matters is appraised value, and spend their time looking at comparable sales, driving around, and talking to neighbors and agents and brokers. Which is OK.

However, this is the core difference between Data-Driven Dad vs. Opinion Dad. Data-Driven Dad would never even write an offer or contract in the Block Group with a forecast value of (-25%). And he would never even look at the appraised value or waste his resources on the appraisal. While on the other hand, Opinion Dad orders appraisals and may or may not win. Their risk is the unknown. Their opinion may be right; however, it may be wrong.

The data does not lie, the data shows only one data-driven answer.

Do you like to make real estate decisions that are data-driven or based upon opinion? These five major myths and misconceptions can cause you major financial losses and lost opportunities. Be aware and avoid them.

Next, before we look at the two Dads; Data-Driven Dad and Opinion Dad, we need to dig into new data-driven solutions, and clearly understand why real estate is - Jacked UP. For many of you, even the most experienced brokers and investors, these will be new concepts.

However, the starting point of fixing anything is awareness of the problem, so read on and become aware.

CHAPTER 2

Why Real Estate is Jacked UP

Why are none of the answers online or offline, and why does no one have the answers? Everybody wants to know EXACTLY where and when to buy, and when to sell real estate, but these exact answers are not online......yet.

Today, NO one knows exactly where to buy, exactly when to buy, or exactly when to sell to maximize their profits, sales, and commissions, because the data to make any of these data-driven decisions, are not available from any Google search, website, real estate professional, or app......yet.

What are 99% of all real estate professionals missing?

Before we reveal exactly why real estate is Jacked UP, and what critical market and submarket data that 99% of the real estate industry is missing, and has no data-access to, first, we need to discuss the basics. The basics of awareness, and how this awareness affects real estate data and risk.

The basics of awareness

Awareness is the first step to anything and everything. What does a fisherman do when he senses a fish biting on his line?

What do you do when you hear your phone ring? What do you do when you sense or see the sun coming up? To start, you must be alive and aware and have a clue to the possibility of understanding.

The Five Levels of Awareness

There are five different levels of awareness, of consumer awareness as described by Schwartz. In Eugene Schwartz's groundbreaking book "Breakthrough Advertising," he listed the five levels of customer awareness as:

- Level #1: The Most Aware: The individual knows your product or service.
- Level #2: Product-Aware: The individual knows what you sell.
- Level #3: Solution-Aware: The individual knows the result he wants.
- Level #4: Problem-Aware: The individual senses he has a problem.
- Level #5: Completely Unaware: The individual does not know anything.

Today, all real estate professionals are - Level #4 or Level #5

Today, 100% of all US Realtors, agents, brokers, real estate investors, real estate gurus, and consumers, are either in Level #4 or Level #5.   Very few, less than 1%, are in Level #4, and aware that the problem exists.   However, the 1% does not know of any online solution.

Most, if not all the US real estate industry are in Level #5.   Most people are completely unaware with no knowledge of anything except, perhaps, a sense that something is wrong.   Many people know and sense that real estate is confusing, opaque, and not working properly, but they do not know exactly why real estate is Jacked UP.

99% of all real estate professionals are in Level #5 – Completely Unaware

It is estimated that over 99% of the US real estate industry is Completely Unaware.   That is why real estate is Jacked UP. The industry is unaware that current monthly and quarterly economic and demographic data is available to them, to make smarter location-based decisions, more commissions, and more profits.   They are not even aware that accurate local and submarket real estate forecasts truly exist. And this complete lack of awareness is one of the fundamental reasons why real estate is Jacked UP today.

Let me prove it to you

Most real estate professionals agree that the biggest drivers of real estate growth are related to economic growth and population growth. No matter what source you use, economic and population factors are always in the Top-10 list of factors that influence real estate risk and growth. Therefore, we are going to use these factors in our three sets of questions below.

Local matters – however - submarkets matter more

Throughout this book, I will be using the words market and submarkets, mostly to simplify basic words and standard definitions of local boundary markets, because most real estate professionals and consumers, do not know about these datasets. These standard definitions are explained more in Chapter 4 and in the Glossary. For some of you, Block Groups maybe a new term, so here is the basic definition.

A Census Block Group, or Block Group (BG) is defined by the US government and contains approximately 600 households. Block Groups are the smallest geographical unit for which there are reliable datasets available. Block Group economic and demographic data is updated monthly or quarterly.

The question of proof

To begin, in your understanding and awareness, let me ask you a simple set of questions. You can use any resource you want, Google, call your agent, call your broker, ask an expert, and call anyone at city hall, even Call-a-Friend....... anything. Use anything and any tool you want to find the answers.

There are three sets of questions. Each question will ask about a Block Group and Zip Code. You can pick the area you live in now, the one you know the most about, or the one your expert knows the most about. Pick any Block Group or Zip Code you want. Even simpler, just research and answer the three Zip Codes if you want.

How to calculate growth

For each of the six questions, calculate the latest growth rate. To calculate the rate of growth, use the simple formula of Growth Rate (GR).

GR, %= (present population- past population)/past pop. x 100%.

You can read up more on this at

https://www.wikihow.com/Calculate-Growth-Rate

For example, if the population in the selected Zip Code is 1,000 in January 2021, and the population is 1,010 in February 2021, the growth rate calculation is (1010-1000)/1000 or 1% growth rate in

February 2021. Therefore, write in "1%" and "February 2021," in the table below.

You have 24 hours to find the answers. Are you ready?

The six core questions of proof

1. What was the GR of Median Income last month in the BG you selected?
2. What was the GR of Median Income last month in the Zip Code you selected?
3. What was the GR of Disposable Income last month in the BG you selected?
4. What was the GR of Disposable Income last month in the Zip Code you selected?
5. What was the GR in Population last month in the BG you selected?
6. What was the GR in Population Growth last month in the Zip Code you selected?

Table #1: Start Here First

Research Core Factors	BG or Zip Code	Growth Rate - %	Date of Data Update
BG Median Income Growth Rate	#:_____	%:_____	Xx/Xx/Xxxx
Zip Median Income Growth Rate	#:_____	%:_____	Month/Day/Year
BG Disposable Income Growth Rate	#:_____	%:_____	Month/Day/Year
Zip Disposable Income Growth Rate	#:_____	%:_____	Month/Day/Year
BG Population Growth Rate	#:_____	%:_____	Month/Day/Year
Zip Population Growth Rate	#:_____	%:_____	Month/Day/Year

Print out this page and put your answers in the table above. Write down your answers. Once you are done, proceed to the next step.

Now put down the book. Do your research and fill in the table above with your research results if you want to play the game and win rewards later.

Welcome back. How did you do? Did you find the answers? The right answers may elude you, because of multiple reasons that will become self-apparent as you read and understand more. First, let me ask......

Can you calculate 1,000,000,000 calculations fast?

To tell you the truth, I do not automatically know all the answers to the questions either. People ask me all the time about what I think about City "X" or Market "Y." And I tell them, well, we monitor over 300,000 US markets. Each of these markets has over 100 variables that change every month. With hundreds of combinations, or geo-clusters that change every month. Therefore, there are trillions, yes over 1,000,000,000 data-points that change EVERY month, and I have all of them, all 100% of all these numbers memorized! LOL!

Image 1: The Problem of Data Age

They say a picture tells a thousand stories, so the below image illustrates the problem of the Data Age and why real estate is Jacked UP.

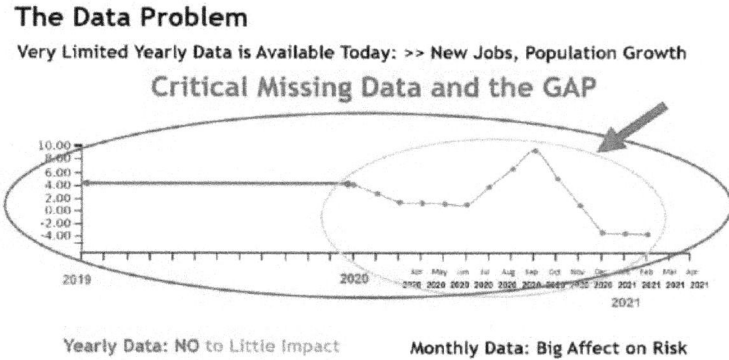

The Data Problem

Very Limited Yearly Data is Available Today: >> New Jobs, Population Growth

Critical Missing Data and the GAP

Yearly Data: NO to Little Impact   Monthly Data: Big Affect on Risk

Table 2: What is and what is not online today

The below table shows what data is available to real estate professionals today and the value to decision making and your profits.

WHAT FACTORS ARE NOT ONLINE TODAY				WILL BE ONLINE WITH APIs		
	Data Factor	Freqency of Updates	User Value		Data Factor	Freqency of Updates	User Value
1	Affordability Index	YEARLY	Minimal	1	Affordability Index	Mo./Qu.	HIGH
2	Disposable Income	NOT AVAILABLE		2	Disposable Income	Mo./Qu.	HIGH
3	GDP	YEARLY	Minimal	3	GDP	Mo./Qu.	HIGH
4	New Jobs	NOT AVAILABLE		4	New Jobs	Mo./Qu.	HIGH
5	Labor Force	NOT AVAILABLE		5	Labor Force	Mo./Qu.	HIGH
6	Median Income	YEARLY	Minimal	6	Median Income	Mo./Qu.	HIGH
7	Net Worth	NOT AVAILABLE		7	Net Worth	Mo./Qu.	HIGH
8	New Businesses	NOT AVAILABLE		8	New Businesses	Mo./Qu.	HIGH
9	Population	YEARLY	Minimal	9	Population	Mo./Qu.	HIGH
10	Unemployment Rat	YEARLY	Minimal	10	Unemployment Rate	Mo./Qu.	HIGH
11	Vacancy	YEARLY	Minimal	11	Vacancy	Mo./Qu.	HIGH
	Accurate 36-Month Forecasts	NOT AVAILABLE			Accurate 36-Month Forecasts	Mo./Qu.	HIGH

You are among the 1% - Level #4 – If….

Big builders and big retailers are aware of the problem. This is why they spend over $500,000 each year on building their own in-house proprietary location-based systems to determine where to build, and where to locate new stores.

If you know how Starbucks determines where and how to open 50 stores in the US next week, and how big retailers and builders determine where to build or relocate, it is not a stretch to understand, what I have been working on for many years. Most consumers and real estate professionals do not know, since all location-based systems with monthly and quarterly market and submarket updated datasets, are built in-house and proprietary.

The individual is left - Jacked UP

Typically, these proprietary GIS or Geographic Information System applications are built using ESRI (Environmental Systems Research Institute) and expensive monthly and quarterly update demographic and economic data that is not "pullable" or on the web.

Therefore, software is needed, because no individual human or real estate professional will ever be able to answer these dynamic questions with constantly changing data. It is just not humanly possible. However, this is what computers are built for. To make thousands of calculations in nanoseconds.

With computers and advanced technology, there are a few real estate professionals who are in Level #4: Problem-Aware. This is explained in greater detail in Chapter 6.

To build predictive models at the Block Group and higher levels, we buy and aggregate similar datasets that the big builders and retailers buy every month at the Census Block Group level. We have built custom SaaS applications and the only custom real-time data visualization platform available on the web.

Note, the fact that real estate data is Jacked UP, has nothing to do with property data, or access to property information, consumer information, or lists, etc. The reason why real estate is Jacked Up, is solely because of the lack of access to current market data, growth data, and local real estate forecasts. Why would lists, or property features even matter to the value of the asset in 6 months? It never has, and never will.

There are some good Realtors and real estate "gurus," websites and technology, and some not so good. But **none** have the **exact** data or technology to know where and when to buy, when to sell, and where to reinvest your profits the next day. Like those professionals who do portfolio rebalancing of stock portfolios.

Our technology will not give you 100% of all answers in real-time either, it is just the first step.   However, it will, if a business blends property data from our APIs, AI, and widgets, that are explained later on, in Chapter 7.   But before we talk about that, let us talk about Dad, and what the two Dads will do.

CHAPTER 3

Data-Driven Dad vs. Opinion Dad

Why quality data matters more than ever now.

What if I told you that you do NOT have the ability to make data-driven decisions - yet.

Today, most of the US real estate industry does not have access to current demographic data, economic data, leading economic indicators, leading demographic indicators, or accurate submarket forecasts. No access to the data that is needed to make smarter data-driven local decisions.

Professionals are left with the option of making risky decisions based upon local opinions and incomplete data and incomplete facts. To better understand the facts, let us look at how the two Dads make their real estate decisions.

The difference between Data-Driven and Opinions

The difference between Data-Driven Dad and Opinion Dad is the difference between standing on a rock and standing on moving quicksand. One stands on facts, knowledge, and power, while the other stands on herd mentality and hopes that the trends will continue and stay the same. However, the real-world is constantly changing. In all large cities, people and Dads (and Moms) are constantly changing jobs, changing incomes, and buying stuff that affects their weekly updated incomes, net worth, and disposable incomes.

Although both men have respect for facts and data, they disagree on how to leverage current data in their daily real estate transactions and location-based decisions. One thinks and will tell you that the data from a year ago is OK and good enough, and just toss in some free yearly data for the entertainment value. The other knows that doing "your homework," due diligence, and accessing the most current monthly or quarterly updated of economic and demographic data and leading economic indicators are the keys to success in real estate.

Some of you, who took the Red Pill, are about to learn how to make smarter data-driven decisions based upon facts and data, and based upon data that has never been available to the public or on the web. If you paused and did your research and filled out the table titled "Table #1: **Start Here First**" in Chapter #2, these next steps should be simple. If anything is confusing, go back and reread earlier chapters and fill out the table. Do your research, then fill-in the percentages, and exact monthly dates.

Data-Driven Dad and Opinion Dad

Opinion Dad wants to make real estate decisions based upon his or other people's opinions.

Opinion Dad wants to drive around, send out flyers and surveys, ask neighbors, search on Facebook and social media, and other more emotional-driven and opinion-driven stuff.   Opinion Dad has a "Job" and as the old cliché says is "Just Over Broke." While Data-Driven Dad leverages current data in all his buying and selling decisions.   Therefore, he has the independence, data, facts, and profit potential over any employee who does not invest and reinvest smartly.

Data-Driven Dad wants to make real estate decisions based upon the more current submarket and market facts, data, and growth, and derives his conclusions and strategies based upon data and facts.

For Data-Driven Dad facts and data matter.   Because even before we start to evaluate where to buy, relocate or invest, the process must start with the best data.   The data is the first step, or the starting point.   The first step is to access to the right data. Without the right and most current data, there is no science, no data, no right or smart beginning at ALL.   First a real estate professional must have access to the right variables…. To the right data.

Today, the right data cannot merely be pulled or datamined because the data is not easily accessible or online. This is one core reason why real estate is Jacked UP today.

How to tell if you are talking to a Data-Driven Dad or Opinion Dad

One way to tell is to ask questions. For example, when asking a real estate professional, what was the population and median income growth last month, in the Zip Code? In Zip Code "X." If they cannot tell you, or instead of saying the truth, like "I do not know." Or say, "I do not know but will get back to you"…but they never do, since the data does not exist on the MLS or in city records. Ask questions.

Many times, Opinion Dads will either say, well, the lines in Safeway are getting longer, or the migration in Florida has grown by "X" percent. But they **ALWAYS** leave off the date. They do not quote the source of the data, as to the last time, or the exact date that the data was updated. Because if they told the truth and reveal the exact date and how OLD the data is, they are quoting, their inaccuracies and lies would be exposed.

When exact dates are left off, it is a good "tell" sign that you are talking to an Opinion Dad. Someone who is only using old stale data and many times using data that is two to three years old. So, they just leave that part off, because it does not support their opinion.

However, just because you or the real estate industry does not have access to something, it does not necessarily mean that real estate is Jacked UP, or a problem.

For example, I cannot fly to the moon or transport to "Y" or find the last digit of Pi or the real meaning of life.   So, just not having access alone, may not be a problem or the lack of something is not necessarily a problem, we must look at the costs.

What are the opportunity costs of not having data access?   How much time do you waste driving around or looking into submarkets that are in decline?   How much more would you make if you knew exactly when to sell?   For everyone, these answers are going to be different.   However, in my twenty plus years in real estate, I know it is worth a **LOT**.

What are the COSTS of not having access to current market data?

Below are different tables, showing what data real estate professionals have access to, in this present day.   The table below shows the before and after.   What you will have access to in 2021.

Table 1: What market data is and is not easily available to real estate professionals today.

What **Opinion Dad** has and does not have access to:

Data Type	Frequency Updated	Total Markets Covered Today
Standard Economic & Demographic Data	**YEARLY**	300,000+
Current Market Growth Data	**Some YEARLY**	300,000+
Accurate Local Price Forecasts	Quarterly	**7,000**
Leading Economic Indicators	**Some YEARLY**	300+
Leading Demographic Indicators	**Some YEARLY**	300+

List of variables and definitions

1. **Affordability Growth** - Takes into account the existing home prices, new home prices, and automatic valuation

models compared to the median income in the selected boundary level.

2. **Disposable Income Growth** – A Leading Economic Indicator and the available amount of money that a household has for spending and saving after income taxes. Disposable personal income is a key leading economic indicator used to gauge the overall state of any given market.

3. **Gross Domestic Product (GDP) Growth** - Is the total growth in the monetary value of everything produced by all the people and companies with the selected local growth market. It is a broad measurement of the local market and overall economic health and activity.

4. **New Job Growth** - Is a core leading economic indicator but must take into account income growth as well. Investments are riskier when job growth and incomes are falling, and less risky when they are both strong.

5. **Labor Force Growth** - Is recalculated monthly for most local markets, is a key component of two commonly used employment calculations created by the BLS; the labor force participation rate and the unemployment rate.

6. **Median Income Growth** - Is the income amount that divides a population into two equal groups, half having an income above that amount, and half having an income below that amount. Median income is a core leading economic indicator.

7. **Net Worth Growth** - Is defined as assets minus liabilities. It is a concept applicable to individuals and a key measure of how much a household is worth. A consistent increase in net worth indicates good financial health.

8. **New Business Growth** - Is based upon the number of new businesses entering a new market or area. Typically, this indicator is a good leading indicator of overall growth.

9. **Population Growth** - Or the lack of it - has a strong effect on local demand for housing. Investments with a strong population and income growth are usually less risky and the combination usually leads to remarkably high growth.

10. **Unemployment Rate Growth** - Is a closely watched statistic because a rising rate is seen as a sign of a weakening economy that may call for a cut in interest rates. Similarly, a falling rate indicates a growing economy, which is usually accompanied by a higher inflation rate and may call for an increase in interest rates.

11. **Vacancy Rate Growth** - Is useful metrics for evaluating a rental property. High vacancy rates indicate that the local real estate market is not renting well, on the other hand, low vacancy rates point to strong rental sales.

Table 2: What current market data is not easily available to real estate professionals today. The blank cells are what **Data-Driven Dad** wishes he had access to.

WHAT IS AVAILABLE OR NOT AVAILABLE TODAY - MISSING				
Data Type	Updated Yearly	Updated Monthly or Quarterly	Metro Markets Covered	Submarkets Covered
Leading Economic Indicators	Some		Some	
Leading Demographic Indicators	Some		Some	
Most Current Market Growth Data				
Accurate Submarket Real Estate Forecasts	Some			

Table 3: Why Real Estate Market Data is Jacked Up

Data Type	Updated Yearly	Updated Monthly or Quarterly	Metro Markets Covered	Submarkets Covered
Leading Economic Indicators		Jacked Up		Jacked Up
Leading Demographic Indicators		Jacked Up		Jacked Up
Most Current Market Growth Data		Jacked Up		Jacked Up
Accurate Submarket Real Estate Forecasts				Jacked Up

The above table clearly shows why real estate data is Jacked UP and messed up. Because the fundamental data to make real estate decisions is not online, or easily available to real estate professionals. As you will learn though, with new data and technology, Data-Driven Dad will soon have access.

If you took the Red Pill, then: What if there was a better and different solution? Would you be interested?

There is a solution in the winds, and that will be explained in future Chapters, as you read on. And show you how Data-Driven Dad can make smarter real estate decisions once the access to this new data and technology is available in 2021.

CHAPTER 4

Five Critical Facts that Google, Websites, and Brokerages Don't Want you to Know.

"When you go in search of honey, you must expect to be stung by bees." — Joseph Joubert

Critical Fact #1

Search engines, real estate websites, and brokerages don't want you to know – exactly where to buy.

Google and real estate professionals will never tell you exactly where to buy or invest in real estate. No tool or service will ever tell you which Block, Tract, or Zip Code to invest in on this day or week, based upon current market data or current market growth data.

In the US, real estate buying and investing is missing fundamental datasets and Jacked UP because today, Google searches, apps, and real estate professionals will NEVER be able to tell a homeowner or real estate investor **EXACTLY** where to buy or invest with today's limited data-access. First, before anyone or any real estate professional gets all defensive and huffy-puffy because, some of our current happy customers are well-educated Realtors, let us dig deeper.

Who advises and who decides?

For the most part, most real estate professionals leave it to the buyer to determine where to buy, since most real estate professionals think that making one of the largest financial decisions a person or family can make, is left up to the buyer and seller. The real estate professional is more of a facilitator of these transactional decisions, and many real estate professionals think that the buying decisions are more based upon emotions and "feelings," rather than data and facts.

The fundamental problem of lack of taking responsibility for helping individuals to make smarter and more informed buying-selling decisions, stems from the fact that - current market data is NOT available to real estate professionals **OR** consumers. In the age of super-fast computers and lots of facts and websites available to buyers and sellers, access to the critical market data is missing online. Buyers and sellers are left in uncertainty and Jacked UP by Google, real estate websites, and real estate professionals.

Today, consumers cannot access the data, growth, or facts to make smart and informed decisions at the Block Group level.

What does "**exactly**" mean? In the US, there are over 300,000 markets and submarkets that are Geo-defined areas with fixed local boundaries. The largest boundary areas are the MSAs. Metropolitan Statistical Areas or MSAs are commonly known as metro market areas or Cities, that contain thousands of submarkets. For example, the San Francisco Metropolitan Area, officially known as the San Francisco–Oakland–Berkeley, CA Metropolitan Statistical Area, has a population of nearly 5,000,000 people, according to the February 2021 Reports by the Office of Management and Budget or OMB.

Within the San Francisco metro market, there are five Counties, three hundred and forty-nine Zip Codes, four hundred and twenty Census Tracts, and over one thousand Census Block Groups. Therefore, the total number of markets and submarkets is over 1,700. Therefore, if Google, any app, or any real estate professional is going to advise a client "exactly" where to buy, in which one of these markets or submarkets, would they or you recommend? In which Block Group, Census Tract, Zip Code, or County?

Moreover, why, why are they going to make any recommendation that is data-driven? That is based upon the latest monthly or quarterly update data?

We all know it is location, location, location, right? So, which location?

Which one?   Which Block, Track, or Zip Code is the best submarket to invest in this month?   Which one is exactly the best market to invest in based upon the buyer, client, or investor's risk preferences?   Based upon THEIR wants and needs.

Which one?

Today, no website, software application, or real estate professional can answer this question, without better data and APIs, which is one fundamental reason, why real estate is in the opaque and Jacked UP.   Only with new data and new technology, can there be the possibility of knowing the exact answers, to make smarter data-driven decisions.

It is not the real estate professionals' fault for not knowing.   No Multiple Listing Service or MLS has the right data or the right technology platform.   No one has current economic or demographic data within their MLS platform.   The core data is not online or available through any Multiple Listing Service.

The lack of data access is a major contributing factor as to why real estate has remained Jacked UP.   This state of disarray is partially to blame for the reason why most consumers in the US do not trust Realtors.   According to a recent Gallop poll, real estate professionals are trusted more than lawyers and members of Congress, but less than most other professionals.

Everybody probably has an opinion about this fact on trust, and why real estate professionals are trusted so little, but I assert it comes down to **NOT** having access to the **RIGHT** data. Without access, real estate and real estate professionals are in the dark and uniformed. Real estate data and data access is Jacked Up. How can the real estate professional who genuinely wants to help their clients, help them? If they do not have access to current market data? The drivers of risk and opportunities. When the drivers of growth, current economics and current demographics, are in the classification of the unknown, and not online.

How can an agent or broker help their client without access to the data needed to make buying-selling decisions?

This is the fundamental question everyone needs to ask themselves and all real estate professionals. Once you understand the fundamental flaws, myths, and core missing data within the entire real estate industry, and the solutions as explained later in this book, then you will understand the core question of:

How Can They?

Critical Fact #2

Search engines, real estate websites, and brokerages do not want you to know – exactly when to buy.

Google and real estate professionals will never tell you exactly when to buy in any Block, Tract, or Zip Code.

There are a lot of reasons why search engines, real estate professionals, and gurus will never tell you exactly when to buy, and all the reasons stem from DATA.

There are a lot of real state websites and tools out there. There are hundreds of thousands of real estate related website today, considering that there are over 1,400,000 members of NAR. According to Statista as of January 2021 the Top 10 real estate websites get over 100,000,000 visitors every month.

However, none of these search engines, tools, websites, or real estate professionals will tell you the best and exact time, the exact day or even month to buy.

Here is how it typically goes when you go to a guru, done-for-you investment website, or other real estate professional.

1) First, they give their pitch about their expertise and experience so you to trust them.

2) Second, they give their pitch about either the market where they sell and are licensed in, or the metro markets or MSA's that they think are the best to invest in because of X, Y, Z, etc.

3) Third, they show you some pretty images, videos, and reports, like BPO's, CMAs, Cash-Flow, and property reports with details on the subject properties that they have listed or are selling within the corresponding MSA's.

Then you have to make a decision. Will the Block, Tract, and Zip Code that you may buy or invest in, have the same growth and Return on Investment (ROI) as the average within the MSA?

This assumption, which is rarely correct, and is a part of your **risk**. The risk is trusting a service that has **no** access to current market data or current growth data, at the Block, Tract, or Zip Code levels.

Because as proven earlier by the **Do Me First Table** in Chapter 2. When you did your search and research and filled out the table, you know that you cannot find current market data on the web. However, the same is true for all other real estate datasets and services.

This is why nearly all these websites and nearly all real estate professionals will never tell you exactly the best time to buy. Typically, most will all say, the best time to buy is right now. Which is not the truth, and nearly never the truth, in all the 300,000 US markets.

Why buy now?

There are a lot of reasons why you should buy and invest in real estate now. The four biggest reasons are:

1. Personal and emotional reasons.
2. Tax advantages and tax deductions.
3. Leverage.
4. Wealth creation.

Of these four, wealth creation is the easiest to quantify, since the other three can apply to anyone, no matter what time the asset is purchased or held.

Why not now?

Provided you can buy now, and there is no personal financial reason for not buying as long as it makes financial sense for you. The main reason to not buy is because there are a lot of perceived unknowns in real estate. Perceived unknowns, unknown risks, and uncertainties. What some real estate professionals call, buyer's remorse. The best way to address this, or any fear of the unknown, is to shine a LIGHT. Get more data and facts and new data. Shine a light on the darkness.

Buying right now is the right answer, but this is dependent upon a lot of "ifs". The most important "if" is that, will the asset go up or down in value in the next 36-months? What data and facts are you leveraging and using to quantify your decision? Are you making your decision with the maximum and best current market data and growth data, as a Data-Driven Dad would do? Or are you using stale yearly market data and making your wealth creation decisions based upon more gut feelings and emotions as an Opinion Dad?

To answer these questions….

As a Data-Driven Dad look at the **last** 12, 24, and 36-month historic growth trends of all leading economic indicators and leading demographic indicators as described in this book. Additionally, look at the accurate local real estate forecasts for the **next** 36 months. If all market and submarket signals are signaling "buy," then absolutely buy now. However, in real estate the "perfect" situation is never possible. Therefore, look at growth data and submarket forecasts, as a powerful new tool in your new toolbox.

Why there is no "perfect" set of signals.   Similarly, there is no perfect stock, car, computer, friend, bathroom, or house…. everything varies, and situations and the environments are always changing.   The trick is to use the best data to make informed decisions for your long-term wealth creation.   Moreover, you can only do that, if you have access to the most current market data at the local Block, Tract, and Zip Code levels.   Then you will and can buy at the right time, in the right month, and in the right submarket.

The four ways Data-Driven Dad and Opinion Dad determine - when to buy

Method #1 – Reports

How Data-Driven Dad uses reports

Today, there are limited ways for Data-Driven Dad to get good data, since real estate in the US is so Jacked UP, as detailed earlier. However, Data-Driven Dad still has a few options today. Companies like ESRI, Neighborhoodscout, CoStar, and others do offer low-cost reports based upon stale-yearly market demographics and economic fixed or raw data numbers. However, no company offers current Leading Economic Indicators or Leading Demographic Indicators, except for yours truly.

For instance, some may say, it is nice to know that the report says that the median income in Block, Track, or Zip Code "x" was "y" in January 2019, when you are making a buying or selling decision in October 2020, over 20 months later. However, who of sound mind would say that this is helpful in making a data-driven decision? Especially if they knew that there was a better source that offered more current economic and demographic data?

Who would decide to make a buying decision today, based upon the 10-day, 50-day, or 250-day moving averages of a stock, based upon the moving averages from 20-months ago? That is 600, yes six hundred days ago. **No one**. No one I know of. Especially, if the buyer of the stock could access the most current moving averages that are daily or even monthly or quarterly updated. No one, except for an Opinion Dad.

How Opinion Dad use reports

You have a few options as an Opinion Dad when using reports. If you like printing, one option is to order all 300,000+ yearly market reports and read them. Then highlight or cherry-pick what data points you like from the year or two-year old data. Then focus your opinion and strategy on this stale yearly old data from the printed reports.

An equally "crazy" idea:

An equally crazy idea, compared to printing out 300,000 reports, is based upon what happened to me last year, when a CRE broker called me. Who worked for one of the top CRE brokerages in the US. He called me in July 2020 to tell me about a new commercial listing that he had in New Orleans. He said that New Orleans "has one of the largest job growth metro markets in the US."

I listened to his pitch about the great cash-flow, great Cap Rates, and how great the New Orleans market was. Then, I asked him to email me a copy of the report, so I could review it, plus the data and numbers. The next day, I reviewed the 86-page report that was dated June 1998.   Yes, from June 1998! Do the math!   He was saying I should make a buying decision TODAY, based upon data that was OVER 720 days old.

My jaw dropped, and I did not call him back.   There has to be a better option other than using two to three-year-old data and reports, and there is, and that is with dynamic heatmaps.

Method #2 – Heatmaps

How Data-Driven Dad and Opinion Dad use heatmaps

Depending upon the heatmaps, which are also called data-maps, Data-Driven Dad can effectively use heatmaps to learn and discover exactly when (and where) to buy. Today, there are three types of heatmaps or what is also called data-mapping technologies or GIS technologies. The three types of heatmaps are - proprietary and in-house, free stale-yearly, and dynamically rendered. Most people are familiar with the free stale-yearly types because these types are more prevalent on the web.

Type 1: Free stale-yearly heatmaps are always pre-rendered, drawn, and created beforehand.

Before they are published on the web or used in any report or marketing media or materials, Opinion Dad uses these heatmap types on the web to show stale-yearly data like crime rates, or the growth of some yearly variable from 1990 to 1991, for example. Many websites offer heatmaps of stale-yearly heatmaps like Trulia, City-Data, and Housing Alerts. If you want stale-yearly data to reinforce your opinion, these are OK sites for Opinion Dad and higher risk.

Type 2: Proprietary and in-house heatmaps are explained in greater detail in Chapter 6.

These types of heatmaps are rendered or drawn dynamically on the desktop. They are used primarily with proprietary in-house internal-use-only computer systems. Large builders and retailers use these systems for site selection, location selection, monitoring inventory, and determine where to build, and where to open-up new franchises.

Also, large government agencies like the U.S. Department of Agriculture, EPA, Department of the Interior, and the Military use dynamic heatmaps to help organize, manage, and integrate complex location-based datasets. Large companies and government agencies primarily use ESRI for their dynamic heatmaps, since ESRI has a quasi-monopoly with over a 90% market share of large businesses in the US. Because of this quasi-monopoly and huge licensing costs, we had to build a new third option, which is Type 3.

Type 3: User-generated and customizable dynamically rendered heatmaps.

There are a few simple tests to determine if you are looking at pre-rendered heatmaps or dynamic heatmaps.

Ask yourself:

1. Can you change the image?
2. Can you add weights or rankings to the factors or variables?
3. Can you easily change the input variables and thus immediately change the heatmap images in real-time?
4. Is the data updated often – at least every month or quarter?

The last point, number four, is probably the most important factor. Because no technology will re-generate over 300,000 heatmaps and update their websites every month with these 300,000 new images.   And the numbers get even larger when using hundreds of factors and variables.   Then, the number gets to 30,000,000. Who would make that many updates every month to their website?

To make the thirty million number even higher, add in custom weighting and ranking.   Let us say, for example, a real estate buyer or builder wants to find the top Block Groups or even Zip Codes in their market (MSA) based upon the following criteria, using the three variables of disposable income, new businesses, and population listed below.   Based upon the growth in the last 9-months.   Each with their separate weighting, which in all cases must add up to 100%, because there is no other data or variable included. The sample below illustrates.

Sample Query:

- Disposable Income Growth – Weight 47%.

- New Business Growth – Weight 32%.

- Population Growth – Weight 21%.

Additionally, think about all the other real estate professionals who might have different risk criteria, desires, needs, or scenarios, who would use different variables, LEIs, LDIs, and combinations with different weights.

This would result in more than a trillion, yes, a trillion, heatmaps that would need to be pre-generated or pre-rendered when the data is updated every month and quarter.

A pretty big number, don't you think?

Therefore, if the data changes a lot, at least every month or quarter, and the real estate professional wants to select their custom ranking and weights, based upon their needs or their client's needs, all the heatmaps must be generated dynamically, in real-time.   This is just how the data and technology **MUST** work.

However, this is not an easy concept for many real estate professionals to grasp, because user-generated dynamically rendered heatmaps are not widely known or used.   It is like describing an invisible book.

The invisible book

As stated in the beginning and revealed earlier, most real estate professionals are not even aware that monthly or quarterly LEI's, LDI's, or accurate submarket real estate forecasts even exist. The same is true for user-generated heatmaps. It is like describing an invisible book. Most people know what the words "invisible" and "book" mean, and what an invisible book might be. However, unless you actually "see" one, the invisible book is not truly understood. You must "see it to believe it."

This is why we created videos, so that anyone can see what user-generated dynamic heatmaps are. Discover for yourself as a Data-Driven Dad or skip this, and other new data and new technology, and take the Blue Pill if you want to stay the same, and live in the world of stale data and opinions.

With dynamic real-time heatmaps, Data-Driven Dad will no longer have buyer's remorse, not knowing, or wondering if, when to buy, and what is really going on in any local market, Block, Tract, or Zip Code. Dynamic heatmaps give answers in seconds. Leverage the freshest data and advanced data-driven tools for analyzing and crunching a large variety of economic factors that affect real estate investments for you and your clients. No software to buy, no programmers to hire, and no huge ongoing data costs to keep your data fresh.

In many cases, knowing WHEN to buy is as important as knowing WHERE to buy.   Now you know. Next, let us look at another method

Method #3 – "Driving Around"

Method #3 is the method used primarily by Opinion Dad as detailed earlier.

If you like driving around, just keep doing what you like. You have the right to take the Blue Pill and drive around, and real estate may just stay Jacked UP, it has been that way for seemingly eons. Change is not easy, and especially not in any large industry, like real estate.

Method #4 – New technology, APIs, and widgets

New data and technologies with new APIs are being developed. What we are building is unique and challenging, since it has not been done before, which is why real estate has been, and remains Jacked UP. However, it is not going to be this way forever. Stuff changes.

Critical Fact #3

Search engines, real estate websites, and brokerages do not want you to know – exactly when to sell.

Google and real estate professionals will never tell you exactly - when to sell.

No web search engine, online search, app, website, real estate professional, or brokerage, will tell exactly when to sell to maximize your investments, profits, and commissions.

Knowing when to sell, is one of the most important aspects in all real estate investing or even home ownership. Millions of real estate investors and homeowners have lost millions, some even billions of dollars. Some even all their real estate portfolios, due to unforeseen local economic changes and local market declines. Seeing this pain first-hand, is what drove me, and still drives me, to know what I know today.

If you do not understand this unique knowledge, go back and read the earlier chapters, take the test, and do your research. If I knew when to sell, I would have never discovered the core missing market data in real estate. I would have never built any software, and never discovered **WHY** real estate is Jacked UP, or written this or any other of my two published books.

What drove and drives me - the quest for ANSWERS.

Many real estate professionals spend their time chasing leads, referrals, doing open houses, and other marketing and sales stuff to get more listings and commissions. Since most real estate sales professionals' incomes are commissioned-based. Getting more and new listings is key to any real estate agents or brokers financial survival.

Is the best time to sell - right now?

Many real estate professionals think that right now is the best time to sell. What happens when you call an agent or broker on the phone and say you are thinking of selling your home? It is estimated that over 90% of the real estate professional in the US who do not have any access to market timing data, would create some story, and say NOW is a great time to sell. Because they want to get the listing. So, they can make more commissions by taking the listing directly or indirectly, as a referral.

But is it? Is now the best time to sell your house…. really?
Is it really the best time to sell in your Block, Tract, or Zip Code?

There are a ton of personal financial reasons why people and families might want to sell their home or real estate asset, which we will not go into here now, since these parts have nothing to do with data-driven or opinion-driven decisions that are quantifiable. Or why real estate is Jacked UP. Unless these personal reasons are just based upon facts and data, Return on Investment (ROI), and the right financial decision.

,

That said, what trends and growth data would help a seller or real estate investor know when it is the right time to sell? The simplest way to answer this question is to look at three categories of data:

- Lagging Economic Indicators.
- Leading Economic Indicators.
- Submarket Real Estate Forecasts.

1) Lagging Economic Indicators

In real estate, Lagging Economic Indicators are seen as conforming to a pattern that is in progress. Data that is "interesting" but data that has little to no influence on future price movements of real estate, local risk, or opportunities.

Lagging Indicators include New Home Sales, Home Prices Index, Corporate Profits, and Labor Cost per Unit of Output, and many other sets of data that are updated yearly. A simple way to test if an indicator is leading or lagging, is to run a simple regression analysis at the Census Block Group. Then add in other Lagging

Economic Indicators for the analysis. See if the variable or variables, have any influence or weights in simple regression analysis.

Do not rely on lagging indicators as tools for predicting future local trends in any local real estate market or risk assessment. In all data testing, Lagging Economic Indicators have no "weights" or influence on future price movements or risk.

- Opinion Dad might use Lagging Economic Indicators.
- Data-Driven Dad uses Leading Economic Indicators.

2) Leading Economic Indicators

In real estate, Leading Economic Indicators are considered to point toward future events, and future changes in submarket values, especially in land values at the Block, Tract, and Zip Code levels. Online research shows a mixed bag of a dataset, as to what specifically Leading Economic Indicators are in real estate. Some say that Gross Domestic Product (GDP) is lagging, which is true, if the GDP data is updated yearly at the Metro Market level. The true test to know if the data is leading or lagging, is testing the data in predictive modeling, or even in simple regression models, as explained earlier.

For instance, GDP is a Lagging Indicator if the data is only updated yearly as with most stale free updated data. However, sometimes GDP is a Leading Economic Indicator when the GDP is updated monthly or quarterly as weighting and regression analysis consistently shows. Regression analysis always shows that the GDP at the Block, Tract, and Zip Code levels has a regression weight, thus GDP is a Leading Economic Indicator, when frequently updated.

In Our Analysis

Not all variables we monitor every month or quarter are leading indicators in ALL markets. Some are, and some are not, because time cycles are constantly changing and evolving. In general, the variables or datasets that have the most influence that are "leading indicators" have to do with time and space. For example, population and income growth, has a huge influence on local risk and future real estate price movements. This is especially true within clusters of Blocks, Block Groups, and Census Tracts, for any three to nine-month time-period. However, this is **ONLY** if the data is updated monthly or quarterly at the submarket levels.

Below is a list of Leading Economic Indicators that we monitor every month or quarter on over 300,000 US markets. These 300,000 markets are defined in greater detail in Chapter 11. Leading Economic Indicators are the datasets that matter the most.

They influence risk, opportunities, choice, sales, and commissions.

They include:

1. Disposable Income Growth.
2. Gross Domestic Product (GDP) Growth.
3. New Job Growth.
4. Median Income Growth.
5. Net Worth Growth.
6. New Business Growth.

3) Submarket Real Estate Forecasts.

There is an entire chapter later on about local and submarket forecasts, and discussed in greater detail in Chapter 10, as to why submarket real estate forecasts matter. For now, Data-Driven Dad makes choices and decisions based upon the best data and facts available. While on the other hand, Opinion Dad does not. Who and which are you? A more important question, who do you want to be in the future?

In real estate holding or investing, one of the most critical facts is selling. Knowing when exactly to sell is key. And no one, as you will soon learn, can sell at the right time of the year, unless you or your representative or real estate professional, has access to the right data.

Critical Fact #4

Search engines, real estate websites, and brokerages do not want you to know – exactly where to reinvest

No search engine, app, real estate website, or brokerage will ever tell you exactly where to reinvest your funds the next day, after you sell your property for a profit.

Why this is, is both a combination of data access, technology, and utility. It is not a simple linear decision, even for the Data-Driven Dad, in many cases. Since the data and technology are not online, yet....

When determining where and when to reinvest, the first step is to set up your risk and reward criteria, since there is no absolute answer to any of the 300,000 US markets.

Here is one simple way to look at it Look at how a full-time stock portfolio manager manages and rebalances their portfolios every quarter. This is not rocket science but does take an Excel spreadsheet, the right data, and some due diligence. This is explained in an article by the Investor's Business Daily here: https://marketsmith.investors.com/Learn/Topic.aspx?name=Man aging%2BYour%2BPortfolio&type=4

How to rebalance a real estate portfolio is a very similar process, provided you have access to the right data and technology. Let us look at the set of two properties in two states along with one other possible property you are considering.

In the below table, to keep it simple, let us assume that the trends are based upon the last 12-months. The up arrows mean historically that within the last 12-months the trends were upward, and the downward arrows means that the trends were downward in the last 12-months. LEI stands for Leading Economic Indicators in the table.

Table X: Data sample – what would you do?

The table below lists three sample properties for your consideration. Imagine two of them you own, and you are considering reinvesting in another new property the next day when you sell the second property, or #2. In property #1, you know it is going to go up in value by twenty percent, so you will probably keep it, right? However, property #2 is going to go down by twenty-five percent in the next three years.

What are you going to do?

Table 1: Table of three sample properties, and what are you going to do?

Property	County LEI Trends	Zip Code LEI Trends	Block Group LEI Trends	County 36-Month Forecast	Zip Code 36-Month Forecast	Block Group 36-Month Forecast
#1 - Own	⤴	↑	↑	4%	12%	20%
#2 - Own	↑	⤴	⤴	10%	2%	-25%
#3 Maybe Buy	↑	↑	↑	13%	15%	25%

What are you going to do, as Data-Driven Dad?

What are you going to do as an Opinion Dad?

IMAGINE IF

I realize that many real estate professionals and real estate investors do not have the data that is in the above table. YET.

For now, I am asking you to just take a leap of faith, and just IMAGINE IF you did.   Imagine if you have the data on the two properties you own.   Imagine if you know with **100% confidence** that the asset will go down in value in 36-months by 25 percent or (-25%).   Would you sell #2 before the decline or not?

Ask and re-ask yourself

Some homeowners will not, since like what Investor's Business Daily states about stock portfolio owners, the same is true for homeowners. Owners and investors want to "think" that they made a good choice, and often sell only after the bad news is public, after they are forced to sell by defaults or foreclosures. This is not exactly investing; this is more speculating and hoping.

Some homeowners and real estate investors might sell. However, today, real estate professionals do not even have access to the right data, which is why real estate is opaque, confusing, and Jacked UP. Google does not have the answers, and neither does today's apps or websites to any quantifiable degree of accuracy.

Only with better data, current local Leading Economic Indicators, and accurate local or submarket forecasts, can any homeowner or investor ever make the right holding and selling decision in real estate, and know where to buy and reinvest their funds, to protect their assets and funds.

Critical Fact #5

No Google search, app, or real estate brokerages will ever deliver accurate search results on submarket risks and opportunities!

No search engine, app, or real estate brokerages can deliver accurate search results of submarket risks and opportunities quickly and accurately.

Because there is no search engine and no real estate brokerage has the technological capability to search across local submarkets at the Block or Tract levels, real estate is Jacked UP. First let us look at some definitions. The first step is to know what "local" and "submarket" means. We have to get straight on the definitions first.

Some real estate professionals might get offended and get defensive about some facts and statements. Especially those who have spent years in training, and with lots of letters on their business cards like ABR, CCIM, CRS, CPM, GRE, SIOR, SRS, MBA, PhD, etc.

Note, I would not make these factual statements unless I know, there is a solution, since some of our current subscribers and clients today, are Realtors, agents, and brokers.

So first, let us define what "local" and "submarket" means. Local does **not** mean property data or the access building data in CRE. In data analysis and investment analysis, "local" and "submarkets" have fixed boundaries. Geographical boundaries that are "local" by definition, are small in size. No one thinks that city data or state data is "local" right?

What is local, and what are submarkets?

Before we jump into the ways of leveraging local and submarket data and analytics, let's first talk about what "local" and "submarkets" are, with some definitions. Below is an overview of what "local" is and some definitions. Here is an overview:

Table 2: What is "Local" and "Submarket" – An Overview.

Geo-Boundary	Definition
MSA	There are **392** Metropolitan Statistical Areas or MSAs in the US that cover only 86% of the US. MSAs typically have a **20% to 900%** error, compared to local and submarket data medians and local growth data at the Block Group level.
County	There are over **3,000** Counties in the US that covers most of the US, and typically these trends and medians are far more valuable than any MSA trends, because they are more granular.
Zip Code	There are over **40,000** Zip Codes in the US. The exact number is constantly in flux, therefore we do not recommend using Zip Codes for data analysis, but OK for marketing, since most consumers are more aware of these boundary levels.
Census Tract are Submarkets	There are over **67,000** Census Tracts in all the US. Tracts are and highly correlated to social-economic divisions, and economic and demographic data. Census Tracts are also called **submarkets** and are based upon approximately 1,600 housing units.
Block Group are Submarkets	There are over **217,000** Census Block Groups in all the US. Block Groups are also called **submarkets** and have approximately a population of 600 to 3,000 people. Block Groups contain the most current, local, and quantifiable economic and demographic data that affect risk and future real estate price movements. Of which LEI's and LDI's have the most influence on growth and risk.

For most real estate professionals, "local" means near or in the "neighborhood" and the only quantifiable "local" markets in the US that have quality data that changes every month or quarter are: Block Groups, Census Tracts, and Zip Codes. If you are not familiar with these boundary names, or definitions, see our Glossary for more information.

Once you understand these terms, you will see why no search engine, app, or real estate brokerages can deliver accurate search results on any submarket risk or opportunity!

To be able to deliver these results, the search must be able to answer some simple questions like those listed below. Try Googling them or asking any real estate professional and see for yourself.

Ten sample questions that are never answered:

1. What is the current economic risk in my local market? In my local Block, Tract, or Zip Code?
2. What is the current new job growth risk in my local market? In my local Block, Tract, or Zip Code?
3. What is the current median income growth risk in my local market? In my local Block, Tract, or Zip Code?
4. What are the top 5 risk factors in my local market? In my local Block, Tract, or Zip Code?
5. What are the latest growth trends of these top 5 risk factors in my local market?
6. How would you compare my local market growth (Block, tract, Zip Code) to the growth in other Counties, Metro Markets, or States?
7. What are the top Zip Codes for population growth in CA this month or quarter?

8. What was the growth in income in your Zip Code last month?

9. What was the NEW job growth in your Zip Code last month?

10. What are the top leading economic indicators in your Zip Code or ANY Zip Code this month or quarter?

Where can you, or any real estate professional find the answers?

The WSJ, driving around, Zillow, CoStar, Core Logic, Google, the MLS?   Which website, search engine, app, guru, agent or broker can get and find the results based upon current monthly or even quarterly updated DATA?

NONE HAVE THE ANSWERS

But it is not going to be that way forever.   Real estate is not going to be Jacked UP forever.   There is a solution in the future.   It was not, and not going to be an easy journey.   Before we start that journey, first we need to know how the "Big Boys," the 1% do it.

CHAPTER 5

The Secrets of How the Big Player Access Current Market Data Today That No One Else Can.

Many people want to know the answer of how. It is not rocket science; however, the answers are not published because the big players want to keep their quasi-monopolies and power.

Let us take a BIG national builder like Toll Brothers or a national chain like Starbucks, for example. How do they determine where to build or relocate new projects or stores next week?

If Starbucks wants to open 50 stores somewhere in the US, next month, how do they do it?

If Toll Brothers wants to build a complex of 200 new homes, next month, how do they determine where to build?

How do large companies like Target or Safeway determine how to use Just-In-Time software to make and keep their shelves filled? How do they adjust their product pricing to match the local median income and disposable income growth, at the local Block, Tract, and Zip Code population levels?

First - How they do NOT do it.   They do not do it by:

1. They do not do it by using free Google maps, free data, or free software.

2. They do not do it by calling up real estate professionals and ask their opinion.

3. They do not do it by Googling trends, asking friends, or asking experts their opinions.

How do they do it? Do they do it with DATA?   They do it the Data-Driven Way, not the Opinion Way.

Big Players do it the Data-Driven Way!   With current market DATA, and real-time heatmapping technology, and expensive offline private and public DATA.

Here is how most of the top companies in the US do it.   They spend over $500,000 per year to build their custom in-house platforms.   Each of these proprietary systems has an ongoing cost of over $200,000 per year in data updates and software development.   You can build your own in-house system too.   Once you know how the BIG Players do it.   The Big Players do it in these three simple steps.

Step 1: Buy or license GIS data mapping software and learn it.

GIS as you recall is Geographic Information System. You have lots of options. ESRI or Environmental Systems Research Institute builds ArcGIS. ESRI has a quasi-monopoly on the market with over 90% market share of the Fortune 1,000. ESRI is an OK place to start, if you have $500,000 to spend. Prices vary and ESRI charges a lot; over $70,000 plus per year if you want to publish and charge for any of their software products. This is one reason, why most GIS systems are built for in-house use only.

- Cost for GIS Software - $10,000 to $80,000 plus per year.

Step 2: Buy and license monthly and quarterly updated data.

Here as well, you have lots of options on where to buy data. The best solution is to contact the big builders and retailers and see what data sources they use. You can try places like Acxiom then Attomdata and keep going up the alphabet. Most of the data brokers or data vendors do not publish their pricing, so you will have to call them and expect to pay anywhere from $40,000 to $250,000 per year for their datasets. There is NO single source that has all the data, so you will need to contact many data vendors and brokers. Then buy or license the data, for many different data brokers or data vendors.

- Cost for data - $40,000 to $250,000 plus per year.

Step 3: Hire a smart GIS Developer to build your in-house system.

It is not easy to hire a smart GIS Developer. Most GIS Developers make anywhere from $50,000 to $120,000 per year in the US. There are lots of variances, based upon their skill levels, where you are, and where the GIS developer is located.

- Cost for GIS Developer - $50,000 to $120,000 plus per year.

Step 4: (Optional) Build your own predictive model.

As of this time, no one we know of, has taken this step because the previous steps are too hard, time-consuming, and exceedingly difficult to get done right. But if you want you can start this step. How we did it and how you do it is explained in Chapter 12. No data broker or vendor sells historic data, so this will cost over five years of data aggregation. And you will need to hire top PhD data modelers to build and back-test your in-house predictive models.

* Additional data costs of $150,000 to $1,250,000 for five plus years of data.

* Additional cost of hiring PhD's data modelers $100,000 to $250,000 per year.

Therefore, the total cost to build is between $650,000 and $2,700,000, as the below table sums up.

Table 1: The Total Cost to Build

What is Needed	Cost Per Year
GIS Software	$10,000 to $80,000+
Monthly/Quarterly Data	$40,000 to $250,000+
GIS Developer	$50,000 to $120,000+
Additional Data	$150,000 to $1,250,000 for 5+ years
PhD's Data Modelers	$100,000 to $250,000
TOTAL COST	**$650,000 to $2,700,000**

Therefore, the total cost to build is between $650,000 and $2,700,000.

No wonder real estate is Jacked UP.

Most startups and real estate companies cannot build these systems. If I truly understood how hard and challenging it would be to "Un-Jack" real estate, I would have never started or gone down the Rabbit Hole of becoming a Data-Driven Dad and Scientist.

However, it was not in the cards. I became a data-driven entrepreneur because I could see through all the 'trees" and confusion, and **SEE** a **SOLUTION** as a Data-Driven Dad.

Next, let us look at the ideal or the Dream Packages that people want.

CHAPTER 6

The Investor Dream Package

All I ever wanted.

What would be "my" dream package – as a real estate investor?

Before we build the ideal dream package or AI (Artificial Intelligence) investment machine, first, we need to look at the current problems with clear eyes from the real estate investing and real estate investor perspective.

There are many problems for real estate investors that stem from the lack of current local market data because the local market data is not updated often enough.   There is no current easy-to-use system for the offline data that is updated frequently, as detailed earlier in Chapter 5.   There is no data or universal system for knowing where to invest, where to sell, or when to buy for the investor or anyone who holds leveraged real estate as an investment, thus there is high risk.

Knowing where and when, is key to any investment strategy.   Just like knowing what stocks to buy, and when to sell every quarter for the fund manager.   The professional fund manager "re-balances" their stock portfolio similarly.   Real estate investors must also know when to sell losers, before major losses of equity. They must know where and when to reposition and relocating into new local markets, Blocks, Tracts, or Cities, where there are new opportunities. Knowing which Block or Tract, in their select market that has the highest opportunity for growth and future asset appreciation, is KEY.

Problems in submarket real estate investing and risk

The easiest way to look at the risk of investing and holding real estate is to imagine if you owned an 80% leveraged portfolio of 3,000 properties: one property in each of the US counties and holding this portfolio throughout the time-period of 1981 to 2025.

At what times, which month and quarter, would all your portfolio be wiped out?

At what times would only parts of your portfolio be wiped out?

How many times would you have to file for bankruptcy and have your credit ruined?

How would have your portfolio performed during each quarter? Exactly when and where would have you sold any property or added more? In which County and on what exact date or month would these transactions take place? These answers are not magical or mystical, they are Data-Driven. Provided you have access to the facts and the data to make these quantifiable, fact-based decisions.   However, as of today, the data needed to make these decisions, are not widely known or available online.

More importantly, what data and information do you wish you had, to avoid the bankruptcies from being wiped out, in the two large national housing crises', in the 1990's and 2007.   And what about the pending declines in 2021 and 2022 in some markets and submarkets?

What local growth patterns and critical variables would have helped you?

Would accurate local forecasts have helped?

Only by examining all 3,000 properties, at all Block, Tract, and Zip Code levels, and seeing the growth patterns and forecast price changes, can you, or anyone, accurately examine the results and expected results with clear eyes and see the huge risks of having or not having local market data, local real estate forecasts, and data analytics technology.

What about the non-investment aspect of real estate investing, of just flipping notes, mortgages, contracts, and property, are these risky?   Were they risky during the same time-periods?

Sometimes, many investors bought "discounted" properties to fix up and flip, just to find out that all their efforts were fruitless, since the real estate market kept declining, and ended up wiping out all their potential profits.   Some even had all their assets wiped out and credit ruined for seven years. Flipping can be very risky, even if you hold the asset, for only a short time.

Relying on macro data for submarket real estate investing

Relying on purely macro data, data from the MSA, the MLS, and property data alone, has and can lead to a huge risk for the average real estate investor, who invests locally. There will be times you get "lucky" with the herd mentality, and will win, as some Opinion Dads, and assume everything will go up in value. This "hoping" is real estate speculation, hoping that the momentum and trend will continue. For real estate investors, a hoping, or hope strategy is not that great of an investment strategy, because the results have proven to be extremely risky.

Besides, the frequency of data updates, which allows for real-time growth patterns, what else matters is granularity. By granularity, I mean very-local, hyper-local, and submarket real estate markets. As explained and defined earlier.

The easiest way to look at the problems of granularity is to examine one sample market and compare it to its submarket. For instance, in comparing one Zip Code to its submarkets or Block Groups shows the huge errors in any Zip Code data. Errors will always be higher, when looking at larger market data, compared to any smaller market data.

Most real estate website primarily want to just sell stuff, get leads, or traffic so that they can sell advertising. They do not particularly want to help the buyer make fast smart decisions, their goals are to sell advertising, not help the real estate investors or buyers.

Some GIS companies have the technical capability to help the average investor make sense of current monthly updated submarket datasets if they were to offer quality data visualization technology to the investor. However, this would cause their main products to be cannibalized. That is, their current income and revenues from their existing product lines would be reduced.

Therefore, because there is no single source that compiles and aggregates current local demographic and economic data, that can, or will, help the real estate investor, investors are left to their own devices, and at times, at huge risk. This is one reason why so many late-night TV shows and "gurus" have popped up to fill the void of the missing datasets and missing information.

However, none of these "gurus" offer any new datasets either, just some non-innovative techniques. Most "gurus" focus on lots of sales pitching and marketing of their products. And again, manipulating the uniformed and the Opinion Dads. Most investors who do sign up, get little benefit from the real estate training, since the training does not offer any new or unique datasets to help the real estate investor.

What is the ideal solution?

All I ever wanted was to be an effective real estate investor. If I save up $10K or $100K, I would like to know where exactly to invest this cash in a good property or asset with a 90% leverage, or 90% CLTV loan, to get a higher and safe Return on Investment.

Assuming terms are mostly consistent across the US, and in nearly ALL cases appreciation trumps cash-flow, this means knowing which markets, and submarkets **WILL** have the highest and safest submarket real estate forecast.

Today, in 2021, this simple question is impossible to answer. Because, current market data, current local economic data, and current local demographic data, is NOT online. And with no accurate local market forecasts, the real estate industry is left in a fog of unknowns and Jacked UP.

The "dream package" is what I have always wanted. The ability to invest smartly and wisely based upon current facts and data. Today, in 2021, this is impossible because real estate is Jacked UP. But hopefully, it will not be that way forever. The answer can be derived in a few seconds with software. (Not our software yet, since we only have some of the core missing pieces of the puzzle).

Pre step.

Determine what variables or factors you want to use. As a real estate investor, I care about expected real estate appreciation the most, so in the below STEPS, I am going to use the 36-Month Block Group Forecasts, but you can change this variable to any variable or situation you want, based upon your risk tolerance, data, or your client's needs.

The ideal solution should have only a few simple steps. Below is a simple four-step process. Pretty easy to do, once real estate is UN-Jacked and new current market growth data is available to investors and the real estate industry.

STEP 1: Determine the top 10 Macro Markets. Macro markets, as explained earlier are MSA's or Counties. Create a table listing their name in one column, and the data in the other. E.g. Expected real estate forecast change of 22.24% in the next 36-months.

STEP 2: Determine the matching Top 10 matching submarkets. The Top 10 submarkets in the Top 10 Macro markets. Submarkets, as you recall, are Block Groups, Census Tracts, and Zip Codes, second column. Add the same ranges of high-to-low ranges.

STEP 3: Do your due Diligence. Test the results against other factors that influence risks, such as the growth in population, new job growth, new business growth, and changes in disposable income. Test current LEIs & LDIs.

STEP 4: Matching listing/foreclosures/properties to the top submarkets after you have done your submarket due diligence.

STEP 5: (Optional): Calculate the expected ROI, cash flow, and equity gain for the 36-months.

The results of the above steps will tell you exactly where in the US you can find the top macro and matching submarkets, along with matching properties in a few seconds, once set up properly. No driving, no wasted time, no mess. The results are Un-Jacked. Real estate will no longer be Jacked UP, with the right data and the right system for investors.

Another more creative option is discussed in later chapters, which is to have a widget and APIs to your investor website.

Note: Hope is not a strategy

Most "Done for You" (DFY) investment services sort of do parts of the above Steps. But they all fail at Steps 2 and 3, which are the most important Steps. Investors are left "hoping" that the macro trends, or the trends of the MSA, Metro Market, or large city, are the same for their local market, at the Block, Tract, or Zip Code.   Hope is NOT a strategy.

Next let us look at the ideal package for the Realtor, who wants to be successful too.

CHAPTER 7

The Agent and Broker Dream Package

All I ever wanted.

What would be "my" dream package – as an agent representing investors and buyers?

All I ever wanted while searching in the four states where I have gotten my real estate license in, was to have a solid and dependable method that was quantifiable and dependable to help my clients, buyers, and fellow real estate investors.

However, I could not find it.   I could not find any dream package or method.

I remember way back in 2018 when my software salesperson was calling the top residential brokerages in the US.   We had many web meetings with the top US brokerages and discussed and demoed our unique market data and software with these firms, including some of their top Chief Technical Officers, or CTO's.

After the 30 to 60-minute presentations and our question and answer sessions, the CTO's main objections were that our software did not directly help their agents and brokers directly make more commissions. They were only interested in software and data that would directly help their agents and brokers make more commissions.

They wanted to keep the customer and their agents and brokers in the DARK and uniformed. To keep real estate Jacked UP, they wanted the industry and buyers and sellers, to remain as opinion-driven, and unclear. Because this way the buyers and sellers would remain uninformed, and real estate would remain Jacked Up, and the brokerage would remain in control.

They did not want more current data that gave buyers more tools to make smarter choices with less risk. As a "Data-Driven Dad," it became my mission to fix this fundamental problem to get those who choose access, the choice of data access.

As a data-driven real estate professional, I know that there is no single source of national or submarket data or any aggregator for submarket data, for the buyer, seller, investor, or real estate professional. No single website or platform that aggregates all the data and information needed to make smart buying and selling decisions for any real estate market or submarket. No single source, technology, solution, aggregator, syndicator, or platform has an effective solution to help the real estate investors, buyers, agents, brokers, or any real estate professional.

Why this problem persists with today's technological advance systems, it is something that is not a linear or clear, but in my dream package, real estate is UN-Jacked, and clear.

My dream package as a licensed agent representing investors would give me access to access a package that would be based upon the individual's wants/desires/needs and deliver an interface with outputs (results of the query) in a fast and easy to use UI, so that I can help my clients **AND** also make commissions fast.

My dream package is not complex.

I just want to be able to make queries and get answers, to help people.

As of today, no such User Interface or UI or technology exists. Real estate professionals are left in a fog of being disingenuous and "salespeople." When asked basic questions like, where to buy and when to sell....

And typically, real estate professionals are forced to leave these decisions up to the homebuyers or investors. More like licensed Uber drivers, that chauffeur the buyer around once they have found a property.

I would want a package with a slick dashboard and UI that lets me "cherry pick," to show off my "expertise" and authority. Not having my client go to some other website and show "me" about the local data, trends, growth, and facts. Or my client telling me information that as a licensed professional I should know or at least have access to the right data. With the right data and technology, I am the "go-to" person for local advice, knowledge, and facts. With facts and data at my fingertips that the buyer (or rider) cannot get from an Uber driver or Taxi driver.

What would be the dream package for a real estate professional?

Most agents and brokers only care about their income and commissions, let us be straight, and think of the process as something like: Lead Gen >> Filter (Contact Show & Tell) >> Get Listing / Lead / Referrals / Open Houses, etc. >> Sell

But simply relying on a system of "leads" does NOT work effectively, and this is one reason why most new agents fail. Some real estate professionals pay over $500 per month, just for Smart Zippy leads. What is needed is a system that everyone can trust that is backed by science and data. That gives the agent and broker real local market authority, and with tools that are emotionally appealing for both the Realtor and their clients.

Simple yet profound.

We have found something quite simple that could change the world of selling real estate and the ramifications are profound. One way to illustrate this, is by looking at how decisions are made.

We categorize buyers and sellers, Realtor's clients, into two main categories: emotional-driven and data-driven. That is, there are two basic types of buyers and sellers who make up their decisions either based on feelings and emotions or based upon facts and data.

In emotional selling, that is, selling to opinion-driven buyers and sellers, agents and brokers use words like:

- Everyone loves this neighborhood
- You want a beautiful house, right?
- It has a charming new kitchen.

Today, fact-based selling, to the data-driven buyers and sellers are more based upon the MSA or state trends, for example:

- San Francisco is one of the top markets for "x."
- Florida has the highest migration rates in the US.
- Phoenix is booming, so put your offer in right away

But what if.

What if the agent or broker could offer the data-driven decision-maker more powerful, current, and relative data? Moreover, before you just spout out facts, data, and statistics first ask your client or potential client some questions.

What current local data matters most to you?

For instance, ask, do you think that population growth, new job growth, or income growth is important in where you are going to buy? Ask them and find out. Ask and re-ask and find out what is important to them or have a fill-in questionnaire form ready and on-hand. Get their feedback and buy-in **first**. Then let your client know that you can, and uniquely help them find the best markets and submarkets based upon the most current local data and trends that **they want**, that fits their bill and needs.

Then instead of offering the data-driven buyer the exact same generic nonsense that every other agent and broker is offering or saying, you offer true location-based **value** and data. You can instantly offer the data-driven buyer answers to core questions like:

- What are the top Zip Codes for New Job Growth in San Francisco?
- What are the top Blocks in Florida for Disposable Income?

- What are the top Zip Codes in Phoenix for Mitigation?

Moreover, what if you are selling to a data-driven decision-maker, who wants to know the latest local facts and data?

What if you could provide the answers to him or her in a snap? Would you make more sales?

What if you could send alerts to strategic buyers? Not just generic alerts about a new listing in your MLS, or a big random list of foreclosures, but strategic and targeted feeds of properties based upon an individual buyer's persona and pre-set submarket, market, or state parameters. You set this up, you or new AI does it, as explained later.

For example, let us say, that the decision-maker wants to find the top three properties for sale in Florida, based upon the same three factors and weights used in Chapter 4. As you recall these criteria and weights were based upon:

- Disposable Income Growth – Weight 47%.
- New Business Growth – Weight 32%.
- Population Growth – Weight 21%.

Now, once you have set up the query and weights for your client, next, simply add in the matching properties from your MLS or CoStar, that will result in the following sample table.

Table 1: Combine properties with custom weighted searches

	Price	Address	Total - Custom Ranking	Disposable Income Growth	New Business Growth	Population Growth
#1	$		98	19%	11%	7%
#2	$		96	16%	12%	7%
#3	$		94	15%	10%	6%

But wait there's more.

What most data-driven decision-makers want is a blend of both the historic growth, the growth in the last six to nine months of key indicators. For instance, the growth in income and population, blended with the expected submarket forecast or expected appreciation of the asset.

To keep in simple and condensed, we are abbreviating the above column headings. Disposable Income Growth is DSI, New Business Growth is NBS, Population Growth is (PG), and 36-Month Block Group Forecasts is FV.

Table 2: Combining Table 1 with Forecasts

	Price	Address	Total - Custom Ranking	DIG	NBG	PG	FV
#1	$		98	19%	11%	7%	24.89%
#2	$		96	16%	12%	7%	23.65%
#3	$		94	15%	10%	6%	21.77%

Table 2 illustrates how agents and brokers can add in and create their own detailed report. Each cell or box can also link or hyperlink to an exact page and interactive graph as illustrated and explained in Chapter 13. The forecast column or the column marked "FV" supports the reasoning the other columns have an historical growth pattern over the last six to twelve months, so that you can properly advise a client.

But wait there's more.

As stated earlier, large builders who are publicly traded, like Toll Brothers build their own in-house heatmapping system using ESRI. Toll Brothers builds high-end, expensive homes, and builds in areas where the local markets and submarkets have growth in median income and disposable income. They run queries on their in-house system to find the top markets and submarkets based upon the latest demographic and economic data and growth data.

What if?

What if, as an agent or broker, you could do something similar for small builders, developers, and small businesses? What if you offered something better that no other agent or broker can offer? So, small businesses do not have to spend the $500,000 in development cost, and the huge on-going data costs. You and your in-house technology team can build similar systems with our APIs to help small businesses. So that these small businesses or even mid-size builders and developers do not have to spend the high up-front costs. They want to know where are the top submarkets that have the top opportunities for growth and expected appreciation.

For example, let us say, you have a client, a small business that wants to know some facts. They are a small to mid-size condo builder who wants to build somewhere in California based upon the following set of criteria:

- Disposal Income in the Top 10% and over (>) $150,000 per household
- Median Income Growth over (>) 10% Growth Rate
- Population Growth in the top 25%

What are the top submarkets in California?

What are the top Block Groups, Census Tracts, and Zip Codes that answer this query?

The condo builder does not want to sift through hundreds of pages of reports of primarily old stale yearly data. What if you could help them and create a table like the below?

Table 3: Blending property data with custom filtering

	Addres s	Bloc k	Total - Custom Rankin g	Disposabl e Income	New Business Growth	Populatio n Growth
# 1	$		97	$430,000	12%	8%
# 2	$		95	$412,000	13%	8%
# 3	$		93	$407.00	11%	7%

Similarly, you can match up any property to these queries as well, to help the data-drive decision-maker. Match property with the:

- Top Zip Codes for New Job Growth in San Francisco
- Top Blocks in Florida for Disposable Income
- Top Zip Codes in Phoenix for Mitigation

But wait, there's more

What if you are an agent or broker, and blogger, and what to write blog posts about the resent changes in population or migration in your market or MLS area? The options are nearly infinite as to what you could blog about. The growth in any City or Zip Code, or the core datasets that your clients are interested in. Leverage our new APIs and available datasets.

This new system can also sync up new land and foreclosures too, if your client is looking for these types real estate. Real estate clubs and gurus who have a technology person, can also build these systems, when the APIs are available to the entire real estate industry. The "best" system is not yet fully developed but can be.

We do not have this system yet, no one has it, but new solutions are possible.

One other option is to look at how real estate listing are marketed today. This is mostly done from syndications. Some are free, and some syndicators charge fees for getting listings more traffic and eyeballs to their listing. However, keep in mind the 80/20 rule, and that many listings fail, so there is an inherited risk for paying any syndicator or advertiser to get me views on your property listing.

What if you could be different? Not be like everybody else and say, I have a new listing at "x" address with "y" features, but be BOLD, be different?.

For instance, you could send out a press release or message to your list, that you have a new listing in Zip Code "x" or County "y" that has some of the highest new job growth in the last nine months in County "y" AND has an expected appreciation of 18.78% in the next 36-months by experts. To find out more, click here www.YourDomain.com/Widget

And at your website (Your Domain) that has our widget (which we have not built yet but easy to do), your website has a real-time dynamic heatmap that show the latest job growth in County "y." And at the click of a button, like in our application, your website visitor can see the expected appreciation and your white labeled 36-month forecast report, as illustrated in greater detail in the Appendix. WOW your visitors and close more sales.

This is what I would want.
But what do you want? Let me know.

When we launch, our APIs can be used and implemented by trusted firms that blend our data with other systems that have current property data that are "trusted." Then eventually the best system for the industry can be developed and will evolve.

Then real estate will no longer be Jacked UP!

What would be YOUR dream package look like?

Would it be a widget, an app, an API, or what?

Let us know.

CHAPTER 8

Our Competition

Who They Are, What They Do, and the Haves and Have Nots?

We have some competitors, most only have stale-yearly data for Opinion Dads and salespeople as you will see.

Real estate is the largest asset group in the US. Real estate is one of the largest alternative asset classes in the US. It is over $3.1 trillion according to McKinsey. Therefore, inherently there is a lot of technology and service providers in the real estate industry. Therefore, we must have lots of competitors. We have competitors, some deliver valuable and useful data, some do not. Let us dig deeper.

For forecasting, our main competitor is Core Logic, which also distributes its forecasts to other websites and businesses. You may see Core Logic under some other name, listed and not listed. The Core Logic forecast system stems from data from the Case-Shiller forecasting models which are discussed at www.economy.com/home/products/samples/case-shiller-methodology.pdf

What these semi-complex formulas do NOT disclose, is what the exact inputs and outputs are.   What are the variables that they input into their models, and how do their outputs compare to local Block Group forecasts?   They do not disclose the core missing data, nor any of their inputs, since their inputs are primarily free property data with the emphasis put on housing sales alone.   They have no trends or forecasts at the Block Group or Census Tract levels, which as stated earlier, these submarkets are the most important levels to track for risk and opportunity assessments.

Our competitors are listed in the table below, and they include Core Logic, Location Inc, Neighborhood Scout, CoStar, Local Market Monitor, Zillow, the MLS, Property Radar, and others. Opinion Dad has lots of places where he can find data points to support his or her Opinion.

Table 1: Our Competitors

Company	Zip Analyser	MLS	CoStar	Core Logic
Category	Reports, Heatmaps, Forecasts, & APIs	Property Data	CRE Property Data	Forecasts, Property Data, APIs
Benefits Who?	All Professionals	Sales People	CRE & those who use OLD stale data	Investors who think OLD data is OK, and risk managers
Delivers Current LEIs & LDIs	YES	NO	NO	NO
Markets Covered	300,000+	Varies	7,000	7,000
When Data Updated	Monthly or Quarterly	YEARLY	YEARLY	Quarterly or YEARLY
Submarket Forecast Accuracy	98%	None	NA	None

The table shows several firms that provide either market data or submarket data.   As stated in earlier Chapters, firms like Autodesk, MapInfo, and ESRI do have some heatmapping technologies.   However, no competitor offers a web-based, low-cost SaaS product solution for real estate professionals or real estate investors.   So that real estate professionals can make real-time location-based decisions on the fly, based upon the latest submarket Leading Economic Indicators, Leading Economic Indicators, and accurate submarket forecasts.

Moreover, of all the competitors, only Zip Analyser (ZA) delivers the leading indicators - the latest demographics and economics and local forecasts. No competitor offers a web-based product to help professionals make real-time, location-based decisions, based upon the latest local growth and local forecasts.

Thus, there is a huge opportunity for new products, innovation, and collaboration.

Especially with new APIs and widgets that are launching soon.

CHAPTER 9

The Only Ways to Make Money in Real Estate.

There are only three ways or categories to make profits or revenues in real estate.

This is not rocket science or complex. And to keep it simple, the third way includes a catch-all, for everything else. Alternatively, if you want to go down a rabbit hole as an Opinion Dad, just do a Google search, and read the million-plus results from the search engine. The only three ways or method are:

Method #1: Future Appreciation

Appreciation is the change in the value of the asset. It is what people think of as positive changes in equity. Future appreciation is typically the way most homeowners and real estate investors make their "profits" over time, by the leveraged asset appreciating more in value than the costs of living.

The simplest way to look at future appreciation is to look at an example of a million-dollar home or asset.

If you own a $1,000,000 asset and it goes up in value by 30% in the next 36 months, then the new asset value becomes $1,300,000.

Your net worth thus increased by $300,000 in 3 years. Note, this $300,000 is NOT a true profit, but "equity" since this asset is NOT money in the bank.

However, the main benefit of future appreciation is greatly compounded with leverage. Leverage can greatly increase your risk and possible returns. Let us look at three examples or scenarios.

Here is the basic mathematics and how things work, for a sample million-dollar home or asset.

Example #1: Non-leveraged (free-and-clear) asset that goes up 20% in 3 years.

Example #2: Leveraged asset (10% down) that goes up the same 20% in 3 years.

Example #3: Leveraged asset (1% down) that goes up the same 20% in 3 years.

In the first scenario your $1,000,000 asset changed to $1,200,000, which is roughly a cash-on-cash gain of 20% in three years.

In the second scenario, you put down 10% or $100,000. So, your $100,000 "changed" to $200,000 in equity in three years.

In the third scenario, you put down 1% or $10,000. So, your $10,000 "changed" to $200,000 in equity in three years.

Leverage is the key to big gains, but this is **ONLY** true if the asset will go up in value. The number or cash-on-cash return is remarkably high, according to Excel, even higher when you get into No-Money Down deals and creative financing.

No wonder Mark Twain said: "Buy land, they're not making it anymore."

However, in Example #3, if the asset goes down in value over 40% at the end of the third year, for example, what happens to the cash-on-cash numbers?

I am not sure that when Andrew Carnegie said, "Ninety percent of all millionaires become so through owning real estate" is 100% true today. However, a larger percentage of millionaires and billionaires got there through real estate and leverage. Some got there through luck and timing, but with better data and an UN-Jacked real estate industry, it will be of interest to see how the Data-Driven Dads and Opinion-Driven Dads react and prosper.

The risk for most real estate investors and homeowners is the unknowns. The unknown drivers that drive local land prices into rapid decline in values, which can be devastating to one's credit and portfolio.

Method #2: Cash Flow

The second way to make money in real estate is from cash flow. The differences between the total assets debt and miscellaneous cost and the income from the rental unit(s). This is not rocket science either. If your total net cash flow is $1,000 each month, then the asset gets or returns to you $12,000 per year in income. If it loses or has a negative cash flow of -$1,000 each month, then you must pull out of your back pocket $12,000 each year. In some cases, negative cash flow is OK, for homeowners and investors, because other emotional, financial, or tax savings benefits outweigh the loss.

Method #3. Short-Term Profits

The third way is from short-term profits, which is a hodgepodge of the rest, which includes making commissions, fees, flips, and other miscellaneous services in which the investor, agent, or service provider has no intention of holding the asset for a long-term basis.

Most millionaires and billionaires who got their wealth through real estate, got there through Method #1 and leverage. This is why knowing the future, or at least have strong data to back up any investment is key as a Data-Driven Dad, and in the next chapter, we will dig into how to analyze predictive models and the future.

The future is POWER, but only if it is backed by data and Data-Driven.

CHAPTER 10

The Knowing - Accurate Submarket Forecasts

When assessing risk, opportunities, and making more profits/sales/commissions, knowing the future and having access to accurate submarket forecasts matters.

When assessing any forecasting model, what matters is their reliability and accuracy, that is to say, can you trust their forecast? And do they show why any market or submarket will go up or down in the future? WHY? As you will discover, today, there is only one company that fits this bill.

Overview - what makes us different?

Zip Analyser delivers valuable insight into submarkets, to help you sell and make smarter choices and real estate decisions. So, your business can automate the decision-making process. No data to buy, no software to program, just point and click. All in one platform, so the investor or agent can look at all submarket levels at one time. Never again myopically depend on just one level alone.

We change hard-to-find datasets into visual information and find "unseen" correlations, to help businesses gain insights and strong strategic advantages. Our proprietary dynamic data mapping software takes a quantum leap in real estate decision making. We have identified the eleven economic and demographic factors shown to have the greatest impact on the future value of submarket and market residential, and commercial real estate. With our 98.1% accurate submarket forecasting models, user-generated ranking technology, and user-generated heatmaps, real estate professionals will finally be able to make smarter decisions, no matter if the local submarket is going up or down in value, in their backyard, or 3,000 miles away.

Previous risk models are antiquated, filled with false assumptions, do not take into account local market conditions or trends, and historically proven to fail terribly. Most critical location-based data is neither online nor available to brokers or investors, in ANY usable format. Businesses need accurate local predictive models, to accurately assess today's and tomorrow's risk. Without knowing the future and what affects local submarkets, all real estate professionals are left uninformed, and in the fog of risk, and Jacked UP.

The first step involves acquiring historical submarket data collected over multiple periods from one or more data vendors. The data categories are comprised of national variables, metro market data, monthly or quarterly datasets, and all Block Groups and higher geo-levels and datasets.

This data is then evaluated to generate multiple combinations of variables which are then categorized into individual submarket datasets and standard databases. These submarket datasets consist of Census Block data, Census Block Group data, Census Tract data, and Zip Code data. They also contain the city, county, metro market, and state-related data.

Each submarket dataset is made up of multiple submarket database rows and columns. This platform provides results that are based on analysis of a vast amount of information. Building a 36-month predictive model for submarket levels requires three times the amount of data as the desired time-period. So do the math... This is why, it took over six years to build our predictive models, and why it is so hard to do. And why no one else has done it.

Our SaaS platform provides a 36-month submarket forecasts. It uses a predictive engine that analyzes the individual submarket datasets using multiple mathematical processes to provide results with high statistical confidence. The following measures are taken to enhance the accuracy of the predictions.

• Different methods or combinations of mathematical processes are tested to enhance the predictive models.

• The methods are re-tested every week, month, or quarter to enhance the accuracy of the predictive engine.

• Also, the expert system comprises over a hundred submarket rules, formulated over time to optimize the forecasts.

Following real estate trends is not enough

Real estate markets never stay the same.   Winning strategies always rely on something new and change.   So why would you use old data?   Or use inaccurate submarket forecasts?

For most, forecasting real estate markets depends on the annual reporting of economic and demographic indicators. But last year's trends are not today's opportunities.

Outdated information limits your expertise, efforts, and investments, thus resulting in lost time, energy, and money.

Problems of macro forecasts and real estate investing

The biggest problem with macro forecasts is their true accuracy at the real local and submarket levels.   Submarket or Block Group forecasts will always be more "accurate" than even Zip Code forecasts.   For example, the average forecast or expected change in value for a Zip Code is -4.8% over the next 36-months.   But within the same time-period, some of the 37 Blocks within the Zip Code will decline by 27.92% and some Blocks will go up in value by 5.88%.

There is always a huge range and dissimilar trends within any large group or market. The key is knowing the facts when you are buying or selling. Therefore, it must be noted that Block Group data is always more accurate than any higher market level data, especially more accurate than the City or MSA data.

Even IF metro market forecasts were 100% accurate

Even if any MSA forecast, or even if any national forecasts were 100% accurate, these forecasts can still be off by 800%, compared to any accurate 36-month submarket or Block Group forecast. This fact is intuitive, but not easy to quantify for everyone. The huge error has to do with the fact that real estate and populations are remarkably diverse.

The only way any large area median could ever be accurate is that all the houses and people were **ALL** homogenous. That is, they are all the same. Think in terms of income or education, or square footage, or age. The median of any large metro market area compared to the highs and lows, at the Block Group level is off by 20-800% for the demographic and economic datasets, the same is also true for forecasts. Therefore, this is why accurate submarket data information and forecasts are so important and valuable to the real estate industry, and data-driven decision making.

Why local forecasts matter!

Even holding the wrong asset in the right MSA can be devastating to any investor or portfolio. This was clearly demonstrated in the S&L crisis in 1990's, and in the recent housing crisis. In our last housing crisis, in September 2007 national prices declined by over 22% percent in three months, and many local markets declined by over 50% in the exact same three months. This observation is not based upon published data, but our data lookup in fact. Moreover, what most people and investors do not know, is that these declines are happening almost all the time in most large MSAs today. Risk and opportunities are always prevalent and changing.

The overall characteristics of diversity.

Some investors do not understand why there can be so much fluctuation in real estate forecasts within any MSA. The easiest way to show and illustrate these variances, is by showing how a core variable like median income varies. Because most people and investors know that the change in median incomes is a Leading Economic Indicator, and in many cases, has a direct impact on real estate prices today and in the future.

In real estate, it is – Location Location Location. It is **NOT**: Property Property Property. And this is why the most current and most local market data, is the most critical when assessing risk and forecasts.

How We Do It

Over 10,000 hours of research, development, and testing were invested in creating our weighted and predictive forecast models. First, we aggregated years of monthly datasets from many reliable sources. We then built and tested different predictive models on over 300,000 markets and submarkets with combinations of advanced mathematical processes.

The result was the identification of eleven combined economic and demographic factors that have the greatest impact on future property values and risk. This backend powers our unique technology, capable of delivering accurate local forecasts, and the "reasons why" any local market **WILL** go up or down, in the future. A picture is worth a thousand words, seeing the future in a real-time heatmap, is worth more!

We aggregate years of monthly datasets from eleven+ reliable data brokers and sources (e.g.: FFIEC, BLS, Analytics firms, etc.). We overlay the maps with many monthly variables like income growth, risk, new jobs index, population changes, and others. As described in more detail earlier.

We then built and tested different predictive models on over 300,000 local markets with combinations of advanced mathematical processes. This powers our unique technology, capable of delivering accurate local forecasts and the "reason why" a local market WILL go up or down in the future. We then deliver this in a fast and easy to use graphic interface data-mapping format. And now, with new APIs, we can also deliver customized reports to a specific client's portfolio needs. Additionally, you or your tech person can build your unique custom reports with the new APIs, which include local forecasts and graphs of the latest data and forecasts.

All future value models have an accuracy of 98% or better. We have 36-Month forecasts for the following levels.

1. National Forecasts.
2. 376 Metro Market (MSA) Forecasts.
3. 3,000 County Forecasts.
4. 40,000 Zip Code Forecasts.
5. 67,000 Census Tract Forecasts.
6. 211,000 Block Group Forecasts.

And coming soon, adding Property Data. With our new APIs, you or technology team of API developers can add in standard property datasets.

Then, finally, we put all these pieces together in one platform and displayed the outputs in easy to use and understandable heatmaps. Our data-maps are rendered dynamically, that is, they are created on the fly, based upon your custom query for yourself or your client.

Identify variables most important to real estate investors.

The ultimate variable list used in our Comprehensive Real Estate Forecast Reports was derived through extensive mathematical testing and sensitivity analysis. Sensitivity analysis determines how different values of an independent variable affects a particular dependent variable (in this case future value of a property) under a given set of assumptions....

By testing each variable in the dataset, we were able to determine which variables have a consistent influence on the models, resulting in the eleven key variables used in our forecast models.

These monthly and quarterly undated factors include:

1. Affordability Growth.
2. Disposable Income Growth.
3. Gross Domestic Product (GDP) Growth.
4. New Job Growth.
5. Labor Force Growth.
6. Median Income Growth.

7. Net Worth Growth.

8. New Business Growth.

9. Population Growth.

10. Unemployment Rate Growth.

11. Vacancy Rate Growth.

We combine these core eleven variables every month or quarter to get our 12, 24, and 36-month forecasts that have a back-tested 98.1% accuracy.   With accurate local forecasts and leading economic indicators, real estate professionals and investors can limit their risk by assessing the latest growth and forecasts, both locally and regionally.

Our real estate forecast accuracy

Our forecasting system tested hundreds of variables to find the ones that best predicted the movement in the future prices of home values.   For over four years, we have backtested the system to improve the results and improve the probability accuracy ranges. Typically, it takes over four years of monthly Census Block Group data to develop a 36-months Census Block Group forecast with backtested accurate ranges.

Accurate forecast models are built in a similar manner and process.

Most MSA Forecast Models use simpler linear processes, and do **NOT** take into account current monthly or quarterly demographic and economic data **OR** growth data. Like, for example, the monthly changes in populations, median income, or disposable income, at the Census Block Group. Some companies like Core Logic, Moody's, Local Market Monitor, and Neighborhood Scout have inaccurate forecast models at the local submarket levels. The comparison table below shows how we compare to our competition today.

Table 1: Our forecast competition and accuracy

Company	Zip Analyser	Neighborhood Scout	Local Market Monitor	Core Logic
Submarket Forecast Accuracy	98%	80%	NOT Disclosed	NOT Included
MSA Forecast Accuracy	98%	80%	Not Disclosed	98%
Number Markets Covered	300,000+	300,000+	400	7,000
LEI's, LDIs, and why markets has gone up or down - Included	YES	NOT Included	NOT Included	NOT Included

Our accuracy - Block Group and national forecast models

A comparison of past predictions against true values over the last 36-months has resulted in an assignment of confidence numbers to our forecasts. The accuracy ranges from 0.986% to 4.065%, which is roughly the same as 98% accuracy. Moreover, our accuracies are constantly improving.

Table 2: Our Accuracy

	Census Block Group Level	Census Tract Level	County Level	State Level	National Level
Accuracy of 25% of locations	0.986%	0.618%	0.558%	0.318%	0.307%
Accuracy of 50% of locations	1.871%	1.261%	1.088%	0.712%	0.527%
Accuracy of 75% of locations	2.426%	2.019%	1.731%	1.099%	0.801%
Accuracy of entire set	4.065%	3.608%	2.913%	1.678%	1.279%

Our forecast models take into account all changes over time at the Census Block Group, Census Tract, Zip Code, County,

145

Metropolitan Statistical Area (MSA), State, and National levels. Only by looking at all these models and levels over time and instantaneously, can these accurate local submarket real estate forecast models be thoroughly tested and developed.

Some people ask, me where do we get our data, so here it is.

We get our data from 3 main categories:

A.   Government Sources.

B.   Industry Trade Associations.

C.   Private Sources.

No Block Group data is available via data feeds, or pullable as stated earlier.   None of the data we aggregate is free or pullable or easy to obtain on the web.   This is part of the reason why real estate in the US is Jacked UP.   However, that is about to change. And, time-willing, all real estate professionals and individuals will greatly benefit.

The benefits of accurate submarket real estate forecasts

- Dynamically spot cool and hotspot segments within any market or submarket.

- Make smarter real estate investments and greater profits.

- Eliminate the guesswork and manual labor to accurately determine the historic growth over the last 12-months, and price forecasts.

- Predict emerging markets and submarkets trends to give you a competitive advantage.

- Discover your true risk and expected ROI.

Additionally, we also have the deepest coverage in terms of local insights down to the Block Group, Census Tract, and Zip Code levels. We offer unique and compelling insights, such as:

- Growth patterns.

- Custom real-time generated heatmaps.

- Custom real-time generated reports.

- Custom filtering and geo-targeting.

- And coming soon – new APIs and widgets

At Zip Analyser, we focus on growth patterns and what **WILL** affect future price changes. Anyone can dump data into a form and show static data or snapshots of the present, or from two-years ago. What matters in real estate is the most recent growth for the last three, six, and twelve months, and the expected future growth, and how this growth has and **WILL** affect future price changes.

That is the gamechanger, as you will see in the next Chapter.

CHAPTER 11

Game-Changing New Technology and Data Access in 2021.

"Data is the new oil. It's valuable, but if unrefined it cannot really be used." Clive Humby

Soon, gamechanging new data and technology will change the real estate game, and "UN Jack" the real estate industry. No app that just changes user interfaces alone will ever UN-Jack real estate or change much.

To UN-Jack real estate, it will take both new data and new technology, not just one, but BOTH.   Data access does exist as we have stated in Chapter 6, the Big Boys have access. However, no free app or simple technology will UN-Jack real estate. It will take new custom applications, development, and programming, and more importantly, the deep desire from someone to UN-Jack real estate.

To see what the future holds, let's look at what unique technology we have already developed so far. Then look at the ideal solution. Then how newer APIs or Application Programming Interfaces will work.   And what's next for the future, because only in the future, will real estate be truly UN-Jacked.

Introduction to secret sauce

We have a special secret sauce blend of monthly and quarterly updated economic and demographic data, the most current Leading Economic Indicators or LEI's and Leading Demographic Indicators or LDI's and local submarket real estate forecasts available today. Thus, we are the only company that can deliver the most current growth data and local real estate forecasts, because we buy and aggregate very hard to find data that is not online or "pullable." We have built very sophisticated algorithms with over 5 years and over 10,000 hours of product development and testing. We have some incredibly special secret sauce inside.

How our current data and technology works

We focus on critical data that affects local risk that is not available online, or from the MLS, CoStar, Core Logic, or any app today. Critical data that shows you where to buy, when to buy, when to sell based upon current market and submarket growth data. Not based on hope or opinions of someone who just wants to sell. Game-changing new data **AND** technology. Many times, even the smartest real estate investors and Brokers, do not know about critical offline data. However, this is about to change soon enough, and the data will be easily available.

We offer five types of reports

You can view samples of our five types of reports at our reports page on our website. Once you log in, you can search any submarket, market, or Zip Code in the search bar, to see the latest LEIs and LDIs, for the County or MSA you selected and signed up for.

Type 1: Market Intelligence Report

These reports are amazingly powerful tools for client meetings, listing presentations, making site selections, and smarter buying and selling decisions. The Market Intelligence Report provides a quick custom solution for your market data needs. You can choose up to three weighted leading economic indicators. With a custom real estate growth data report, you can request the specific market research and trends you need for each of your projects. We give you the power to choose what bests sells your local market with customizable local reports.

Build custom reports, based upon the latest submarket growth. Build strong custom marketing materials, to grow your business. Serve your clients better and add immediate client value. These reports deliver new cost-effective, data-driven, submarket analytics, and current growth data, so you can get your competitive advantage. Reports are included in memberships. Or you can purchase separately.

Type 2: White Label - Market Intelligence Report

Our white label reports offer a quick and impressive way to get your name in front of potential clients. When the clients and potential viewers see your name on reports, your business becomes something trustworthy and reliable. Credibility helps you expand very fast.

Personalize your reports to fit the needs of your clients. This allows you to create your own custom generated reports, and advertise your products, exactly how you want to — all without spending any time on development!

Save time and money

If you wanted to create your own report, how long would it take to complete?   We are offering white labeling reports that have already been development.   This means you can start with a finished, white labeled reports rather than take the time to develop the technology yourself.

Building custom market reports for your clients can take hours to design and build, even days, or longer.   Creating new custom reports can be very time consuming, is the fact that there is a learning curve when creating something from the ground up. Why waste time reinventing the wheel when you can white label?

White labeling will save months of development time of your team which can be used to boost your business, or you can spend it on marketing work. Another major benefit of using white label software is that the custom reports can be used immediately.

Type 3: Comprehensive Real Estate Forecast Report

These reports are based upon the local market you select, and the time periods you select. Search by any address, and we also include the latest growth data for all eleven key leading economic and demographic indicators. The first page of the report shows the local forecast, compared to the national real estate forecast. All the remaining pages show the latest growth and supporting factors that contribute to the growth or decline in that local real estate market. So, you can see not only the actual forecast or expected appreciation, but also the contributing factors in the submarkets or markets that are growing or declining.

Type 4: White Label - Comprehensive Real Estate Forecast Report

Type 5: Custom CMA or Listing Reports with our APIs

For these last 2 report types see what they look like in our Appendix.

The ideal real estate technology

What is the ideal real estate technology that can help real estate professionals reduce risk, increase opportunities, and make more profits/sales/commissions?

The idea of search technology for real estate professionals is important. What real estate professionals care about most are: saving time, finding deals, buying and selling at the "right" time to maximize their profits, sales, and returns. Additionally, investors care about clearly knowing where to reinvest their profits soon, so that they can avoid taxes, by leveraging 1031 Exchanges.

Today, no such real estate technology exists, since no real estate website has current submarket economic or demographic data, which is updated frequently at the Block, Tract, or Zip Codes levels. No mass market Block Group forecasting system with accurate future appreciation or depreciation exists. Therefore, holding real estate can be a very risky endeavor. Knowing exactly when to sell, is a very elusive fact of the future. Thus, the huge risk remains, until better submarket forecasting models are developed and deployed across the industry.

How the ideal real estate technology can help real estate agents and brokers.

Despite what any commissioned real estate agent and broker may tell you, what agents care about are commissions and systems that help them make more commissions and profits. There are some exceptions to this rule; like buyer-broker agreements, and some hourly and discount brokerages, but still, what matters is commissions. Just like why most people who work for a living or have a "job" – what matters is their paycheck.

The ideal real estate technology will help the real estate professional make more commissions. Some may say that this translates to getting more listing and leads, but this simple answer does not address the fact that today, over 47% of all listing expire, and according to major surveys, over 67% of Americans do not trust agents.

So, the answer is more about, getting the "right" listings at the right price that will sell, and getting the "right" leads that result in getting more commissions, and leveraging the "right" new data and new technology. That is, get "real" buyers and sellers and investors, not shoppers or wannabe investors.

The ideal technology both helps the buyer and seller, and once the buyer has selected the optimal Block, Tract, or Zip Code, and located the optimal listing or foreclosure within the market or submarket, the agent can show the buyer the property, and thus make more commissions. Thus, the true local or submarket expert who has access to current LEIs, LDIs, and accurate submarket forecasts, is worthy of making 6% or more, since they are **THE** Data-Driven Expert.

How can the ideal real estate technology help real estate websites?

To begin any submarket real estate analysis on how the ideal technology can help other real estate websites, we first need to look at how websites today, receive and republish existing datasets.

Most real estate data vendors send real estate websites fresh daily updates by XML (Extensible Markup Language) and RSS (Rich Site Summary). According to Wikipedia - A data feed is a mechanism for users to receive updated data from data sources. It is commonly used by real-time applications in point-to-point settings as well as on the World Wide Web. The latter is also called web feed. RSS feed makes the dissemination of blogs easy. Product feeds play an increasingly important role in e-commerce and internet marketing. Data feeds usually require structured data.

Therefore, the ideal new data and new technology would send the core missing Block, Tract, and Zip Code data from some sort of feed or API (Application Programming Interface). However, the raw growth data by itself has little value and little utility to the API developer or the individual consumer or real estate professional. For example, what do these numbers mean?

"gid": 90010101011,"affordability": "2019q2": "0.02008" "2019q3": "0.02008991008" "2019q4": "-0.1140755044955044955050" "2020q1": "-0.0203149887612387612387250" "2020q2": "0.0732111256836913086918094 0625"

For most real estate professionals, these numbers are meaningless, so a data feed is not the optimal or even useful technology. Any number needs to have some value and utility to be meaningful. No simple data feed of Block Group number 010010201001, the BG number, would by itself, make sense to any consumer or real estate professional. By itself, this number has no value or utility. Similarly, the data feed based upon Census Tract number 01043964400, would not make sense to the average web user, surfer, or real estate professional.

The ideal real estate technology would send real estate portals and websites the freshest submarket and market demographics, economics, and growth patterns via data charts, and GIS technology to make instant sense and visualize these datasets. Then all real estate website and portals can then also help their client base, and build additional products to enhance their product mix and offerings, which leads to additional revenues.

To put it another way, the ideal new data and technology would fill in the data **GAPS**. The table below, for example, shows one LEI, the growth in Median Income for a sample Block Group.

Some cells are marked "Jacked UP." None of this data is online or available to over 99% of the US real estate professionals, as detailed in earlier Chapters. The ideal new data and technology will fill in the missing gaps, or cells, and the entire real estate industry will then have access through new APIs.

Table 1: The ideal new technology fills in the missing datasets for all LEIs, LDIs, and submarket forecasts.

Median Income Growth Rate	3 Months	6 Months	12 Months	24 Months	36 Months	Rating
Block Group	Jacked UP	Jacked UP	Jacked UP	8.93% Graph It Map It	9.13% Graph It Map It	Excellent
Census Tract	Jacked UP	Jacked UP	Jacked UP	8.13% Graph It Map It	8.93% Graph It Map It	Excellent
Zip Code	Jacked UP	Jacked UP	Jacked UP	4.13% Graph It Map It	5.13% Graph It Map It	Excellent
County	Jacked UP	Jacked UP	Jacked UP	3.03% Graph It Map It	4.23% Graph It Map It	Fair
Metro Market	Jacked UP	Jacked UP	Jacked UP	4.33% Graph It Map It	4.27% Graph It Map It	Fair
State	Jacked UP	Jacked UP	Jacked UP	0.03% Graph It Map It	0.13% Graph It Map It	Fair
Nation	Jacked UP	Jacked UP	Jacked UP	0.01% Graph It Map It	0.03% Graph It Map It	Fair

Today, all the above is Jacked UP, but some people may think that the changes from the stale-yearly data from January 2018 to January 2020, that is really only two data points, is a 24-month growth trend. So, to keep those Opinion Dads happy, we did not call these cells as Jacked Up, but as any Data-Driven Dad knows, **ALL** the cells, and data, in the above table, are Jacked UP.

For me, the above, is such a no-brainer, but my broker friend told me I need to explain what I mean by the above two data points.

Between the time of January 2018 to January 2020 there are twenty-four months, right. Therefore, a two-year graph should have 24 datapoints, **NOT TWO**. There are lots of changes in economic data within a two-year time-period.

In fact, there are 24-months for every LEIs, LDIs, and submarket forecast. As stated earlier, people are constantly changing jobs, changing their incomes, moving, and buying things, that affects median incomes, disposable incomes, and population changes every month, **NOT** just in January, for any given year, right?

In fact, everything in the table should say "Jacked Up" since the data and heatmaps are NOT available to the real estate professionals or investors today. Some may say that Neighborhood Scout, Core Logic, Location Inc, CoStar, or some other real estate software provides accurate 24, and 36-month growth charts, but this is **NOT** the case.

How to use new data and technology

Our current technology provides real estate growth data and local forecasts in the form of submarket heatmaps. The User Interface has ranked and tiered weighted searches, where you can generate dynamic submarket heatmaps by using different search criteria.

The dynamic submarket maps are visually represented as heatmaps with five color ranges. Also, you can instantly view, find, and export dynamic maps into a table. For greater convenience, you can slide a spatial slider to generate customized heatmaps. Dynamically access all spatial boundary information in a report, form, web page, or a dynamically generated heatmap.

FYI

The National Real Estate Investor had a report out in late 2019 on how demographics data will have extensive access by 2025, at www.nreionline.com/real-estate-services/technological-disruption-commercial-real-estate

But with new APIs and technology, both demographic and economic data should have extensive access via our new disruptive technology and APIs. With our new solutions, you do not have to wait until 2025. Below is an edited image of this post, where we moved the date, to illustrate these new changes.

Image 1: CRE Disruption Timeline

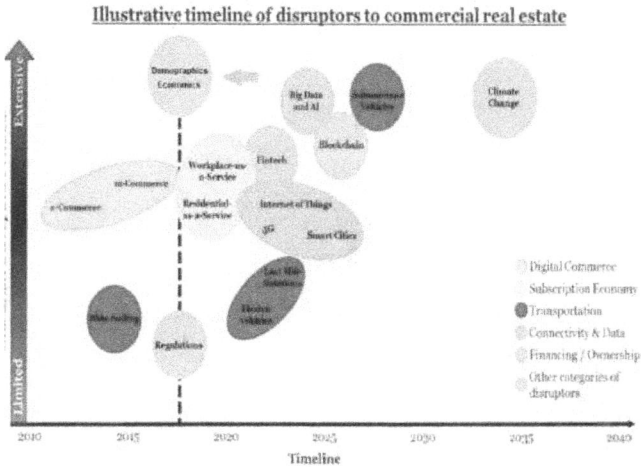

Illustrative timeline of disruptors to commercial real estate

The below table is for illustration purposes only. None of the numbers are real or accurate. This is just a mockup sample table. They are only a placeholder. Hopefully, by now you know that this data changes so often, it would make no sense to publish any actual numbers in any book. Right?

Table 2: The solutions

Median Income Growth Rate	3 Months	6 Months	12 Months	18 Months	24 Months	30 Months	36 Months	
Block Group	2.13% Graph It Map It	2.93% Graph It Map It	1.13% Graph It Map It	3.13% Graph It Map It	0.03% Graph It Map It	0.23% Graph It Map It	0.13% Graph It Map It	Fair
Census Tract	9.13% Graph It Map It	8.93% Graph It Map It	5.13% Graph It Map It	3.13% Graph It Map It	0.03% Graph It Map It	0.23% Graph It Map It	0.13% Graph It Map It	Excellent
Zip Code	9.13% Graph It Map It	8.93% Graph It Map It	5.13% Graph It Map It	3.13% Graph It Map It	0.03% Graph It Map It	0.23% Graph It Map It	0.13% Graph It Map It	Excellent
County	9.13% Graph It Map It	8.93% Graph It Map It	5.13% Graph It Map It	3.13% Graph It Map It	0.03% Graph It Map It	0.23% Graph It Map It	0.13% Graph It Map It	Excellent
Metro Market	9.13% Graph It Map It	8.93% Graph It Map It	5.13% Graph It Map It	3.13% Graph It Map It	0.03% Graph It Map It	0.23% Graph It Map It	0.13% Graph It Map It	Excellent
State	9.13% Graph It Map It	8.93% Graph It Map It	5.13% Graph It Map It	3.13% Graph It Map It	0.03% Graph It Map It	0.23% Graph It Map It	0.13% Graph It Map It	Excellent
Nation	9.13% Graph It Map It	8.93% Graph It Map It	5.13% Graph It Map It	3.13% Graph It Map It	0.03% Graph It Map It	0.23% Graph It Map It	0.13% Graph It Map It	Excellent

ONE MORE IMPROTANT THING:

As I stated in the beginning, my drive and possession is NOT to sell software or books, it is to Un-Jack real estate to help agents and investors.

And to get feedback on what we have built so far. My contact information is at our website, and I invite you to Book a Call there at

https://www.zipanalyser.com/book-a-call/

What does the future hold? Imagine if

IMAGINE IF you had access to better data & technology.

Would you make better decisions?

Be more Professional?

Make more sales?

Better information leads to more sales.

Imagine if real estate was "UN-Jacked."

Delivering more VALUE to every potential client.

More effectively developing and sharing your insights.

Imagine if you had access to better data and technology.

Just Imagine!

CHAPTER 12

The Benefits of New Data and Technology for Real Estate Professionals.

By now you already know that data matters, and having access to the most current market data, LEIs, LDIs, and submarket forecasts matter a lot. They matter the most if you are a Data-Driven Dad who cares about data.

The benefits to any new data and new technology can be enormous, however, the benefits are highly dependent on how you access and apply the data in your daily real estate endeavors and actions. The benefits also vary, depending upon which tool you use, and how you blend new APIs into your existing reports, media, and websites.

Since our APIs do not exactly or automatically help the individual real estate investor, agent, or broker, our API launch is just the first step in UN-Jacking real estate.

All people, all investors, agents, and brokers want and will want different things. That is the beauty of APIs. **YOU** can choose. You can choose what data, graphs, or heatmap images best fit your individual needs, as a fixed image in reports, or as dynamic images on the web, or in your website.

Depending upon your needs, whether you are assessing risk, searching for opportunities, or just want to make more profits or commissions, new APIs can help you. Just choose the data that delivers the facts that you want as a Data-Driven Dad. And you can, like in our custom reports, cherry-pick the API data that supports your Opinion, to better sell your property in any market or submarket. This is the beauty of Application Programming Interfaces, you can choose.

The Benefits:

- Make better buying and selling decisions.

- Increased ROI, sales, and revenues.

- Reduce unnecessary risk.

- Measure and analyze any local housing market in seconds.

- Build strong strategic advantages and grow your business.

- Save hundreds of thousands of dollars on building it yourself.

- Create slick and custom listing and client reports, to close more sales.

- Optimize your investment portfolios, based upon the latest local growth.

1. Dynamic and Immediate.

2. Add Value.

3. Build Trust.

4. Smart Investing and Optimized Portfolio.

What you can do with this point, is get immediate access to local growth analytical data. Analyzing your local and regional markets, matching your client's criteria to your specific properties, whether you are sitting at your desk or sitting in your car.

Dramatically improve your likelihood for success while adding value to your clients. Deliver outstanding marketing materials, whether it is hardcopy or digitally customized to match your clients' priorities.

Build trust with clients by clearly demonstrating your offering, above and beyond, by having access to cutting-edge local data analytics and data visualization technology. When you deliver better data and technology to your clients, and WOW them with real-time customized reports and dynamic heatmaps, your customers are more likely not to stray, while you are building trust and rapport.

With accurate local forecasts, help your clients minimize their downside risk by assessing multiple categories of growth and forecasting, both locally and regionally.

Zip Analyser leads in providing real estate market data that generates success. Our exclusive APIs now brings growth data directly to you, according to your needs. No matter your industry, role, or goals, Zip Analyser's APIs ensure that you are equipped to maximize every dollar and every decision.

Six months is too late. Year-old data ss out of the question.

Data places you in the curve. Precise, real-time data gives you the power to shape it.

The highest-earning and most successful market actors are those who keep up with the technological advances that push the real estate market forward. Early adoption can accelerate growth, while delay can cause loses in earnings and position in our highly competitive industry.

Zip Analyser's APIs are the newest and most reliable tools giving you the actionable data now. The only thing separating you from rest is useful, and current market data. Your tireless work and valuable investments will yield the highest return possible.

CHAPTER 13

Getting Started

If You Choose the Red Pill and the Next Steps.

When real estate is finally UN-Jacked and the data is available to all real estate professionals, you will have a choice. You can be like one of the Three Monkeys and – See no Evil, Hear no Evil, and Speak no Evil, which is a metaphor for staying myopic and remaining a Luddite.

You can stay as an Opinion Dad, or you can embrace new data and technology. The cool thing is, for **ONCE** you will have a choice. If enough people choose the right pill and data, like in anything, or any election for example, then we and real estate will no longer be Jacked UP.

To be super clear, let us look at one more example. Let us say you heard that both Florida and Texas have expected high new job growth and high population growth. Both have the two factors that you think drives prices, and you have heard that these two states, for example, have growth of these two factors.

For illustration purposes, and to keep it simple and easier, let us say that you are considering buying one house in one of the two states, in Texas or Florida. Both houses are new construction and built by the same builder, so the above-ground asset, or the house is the same in both states. And to keep it even simpler, let us just look at just one factor or variable, New Job Growth.

Now let us dig a little deeper with an illustrated example.

In one state, you can see that the Census Block Group has poor ranking and declining based upon the last twelve months in the image below. The Block Group has a Ranking of 373 within all the thousands of Block Groups within the MSA, and a negative growth rate of -9.77% within the last 12- months.

Image 1: How one sample Block Group ranks and the growth data.

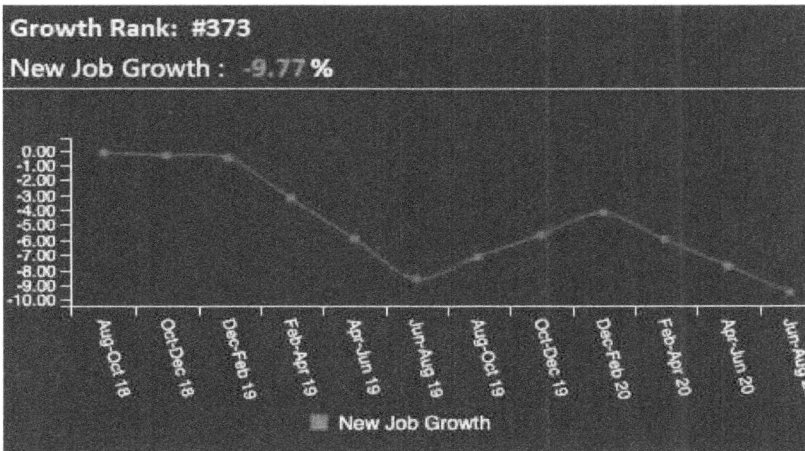

The other Block Group, in the other state, with the exact same cash flow, and the exact same building, has a different trend line and graph as illustrated below.

Image 2: How the other sample Block Group ranks and the growth data.

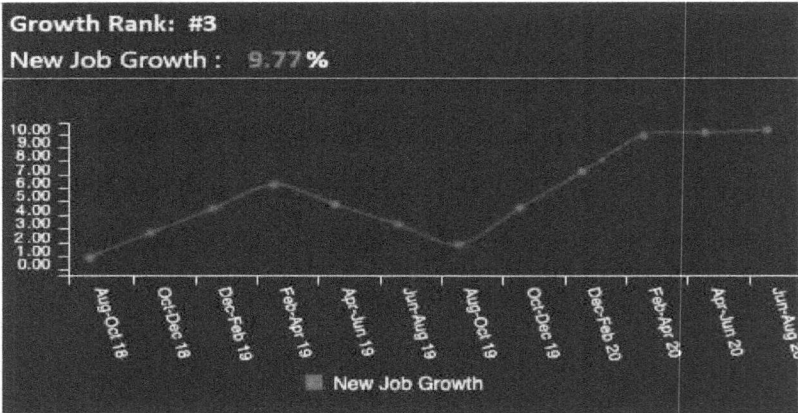

Which would you choose, or write an offer on, if you did have access to the data and real estate was no longer Jacked UP?

Additionally, we are developing and deploying interactive APIs so you can post interactive graphs and heatmaps in your blog, website, or other media.

For example, in the image below, as you mouseover the graph you can, and will see the exact monthly growth rate of the Leading Economic Indicator, Leading Demographic Indicator, or submarket forecasts. In the example below, we are showing the growth in New Job Growth.

Image 3: Sample interactive graph with mouseover

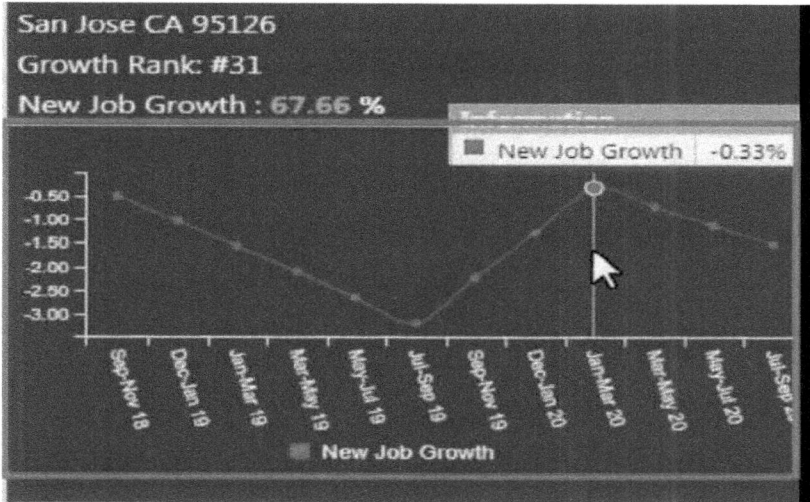

With enough of these interactive charts and partners, real estate could become UN-Jacked in 2021.   Time will tell.

To get started and learn more, simply go to our website, https://www.zipanalyser.com and Book a Call on Zoom to learn more.

In conclusion….

A good friend once told me, that if fish swim in the water, then humans swim in the world of opinions.

That is, we are always thinking, if we are alive and awake, or at least most of the time. :)

With better and more current market data and new technology, widgets and APIs, you will have a choice to swim in the ocean as Opinion Dad or take the Red Pill and be and become a Data-Driven Dad to increase your profits.

The future has choices.

Choose Wisely!

About Zip Analyser

Zip Analyser (ZA) offers real estate professionals in the United States an online data visualization and forecasting platform to gain access to the most current local demographic and economic growth data. The service is aimed at investors, real estate professionals, businesses, and risk managers looking to make smarter, and location-based property decisions.

The founder of the startup Eddie Godshalk has over 20 years of experience in the finance and Real Estate industry and has purchased more than 40 investment properties. Being able to make informed decisions is the key to success in real estate and having accurate local real estate forecasts is the key to informed and smarter decisions.

Since such data did not exist, Eddie founded Zip Analyser to provide it.

Glossary

API (Application Programming Interface) is a computing interface and set of programming code which defines interactions between multiple software intermediaries. Although an APIs is not a common term to most consumers, according to Postman, every piece of software built today either uses an API, or is an API.

AVM (Automated Valuation Models) is a term for a service that uses mathematical modeling combined with databases of existing properties and transactions to calculate real estate values. AVMs are software-based pricing models used in the real estate market to value properties. AVMs are more efficient than a human appraiser, but they are also usually only less accurate than standard appraisals.

Census Block Groups (BG) are defined by the US government and contain approximately 600 households. The BG is the smallest geographical unit for which there is reliable data available. There are 217,000 BGs in the U.S. and Zip Analyser covers over 98% of them.

Census Block Groups are identified by a series of unique numbers. BGs never cross the boundaries of states, counties, or major roads or railroad tracks, thus typically they define the "right side" and the "wrong side" of the railroad tracts. Without custom GIS programming, it is typically not possible to aggregate Block Groups (or Census Tracts) to all other types of submarket levels, to Zip Codes, for example. The Zip Analyser technology blends together all submarket levels so that their levels can be viewed instantaneously. The BG trends are the most important variables to consider when investing and properly assessing risk.

Census Tracts (CT) are clusters of Block Groups (BG) and typically have approximately 1,500 households. There are over 73,000 Census Tracts in the U.S. Census Tracts are designed to be relatively homogeneous units with respect to population characteristics, economic status, and living conditions, according to the U.S. Census Bureau. Census Tract boundaries are delineated to be maintained over a long time so that statistical comparisons can be made from month-to-month, quarter-to-quarter, or year-to-year. Like Block Groups (BG), Census Tracts do not aggregate into Zip Codes, without custom GIS programming.

CRE (Commercial Real Estate) includes office buildings, medical centers, hotels, malls, retail stores, multifamily housing buildings, farmland, warehouses, and garages.

ESRI (Environmental Systems Research Institute) Is the large GIS company that most large companies and government agencies use ESRI for their dynamic heatmaps. ESRI has a quasi-monopoly with over a 90% market share of large businesses in the US.

GIS (Geographic Information System) is a computer system for capturing, storing, checking, and displaying data related to positions on Earth's surface. GIS can show many kinds of data on one map, enabling people and business to easily see, analyze, and understand patterns and relationships.

LEI (Leading Economic Indicators) are datasets that precede economic events. LEIs are economic indicators about the economic activity. LEIs allow analysis of economic performance and predictions of future performance. They include various datasets such as the unemployment rate, housing starts, consumer price index, industrial production, gross domestic product, broadband internet penetration, weekly updated retail sales, and money supply changes.

LDI (Leading Demographic Indicators) are population based on factors such as the local growth in populations, employment, education, and birth rates.

MLS (Multiple Listing Service) is a database established by cooperating real estate brokers to provide shared data about properties for sale. An MLS compiles sales data submitted by member brokers and agents, along with detailed information that brokers, and agents can access online.

MSA's (Metropolitan Statistical Areas) is a geographic area defined by the Office of Management and Budget (OMB). A MSA is a geographical region with a relatively high population density at its core and close economic ties throughout the area. MSA's are defined by the Office of Management and Budget (OMB) and vary by number. Currently, there are 381 MSA's in the US. Often referred to as a "market" which is a huge area, and a metropolitan area contains a core urban area of at least 50,000 people.

Due to the exceptionally large size of MSA's, typically there is VERY LITTLE correlation to the local Block Group or Census Tract data or changes in any local market.

Widgets are formatted for websites and HTML. It can send both technology and data to a website, embedded code, and usually involves templates for websites.

Widgets. Widgets are also cached to load extremely quickly, which means the data is not instantaneously updated. Compared to APIs which primarily take some programming skill to use, and most just send data.

Zip Codes are five-digit numbers established by the United States Postal Service, to identify a location and route the mail to that location. Zip+4 is the five-digit Zip Code, which indicates the state and post office or postal zone, plus four digits as an expanded code that denotes the box section or number portion of a rural route, building, or other specific delivery location. There are approximately 41,000 Zip Codes in the US, and the boundaries of Zip Codes do not typically match with the boundaries of Block Groups or Census Tracts. The Zip Code may split a Block Group.

Appendix

How our 3-Step Search and Find system works:

Step 1: Enter in an Address

Step 2: Select your LEI or LDI and Historic Growth Rate **OR** Forecast Time-Period
and click Enter

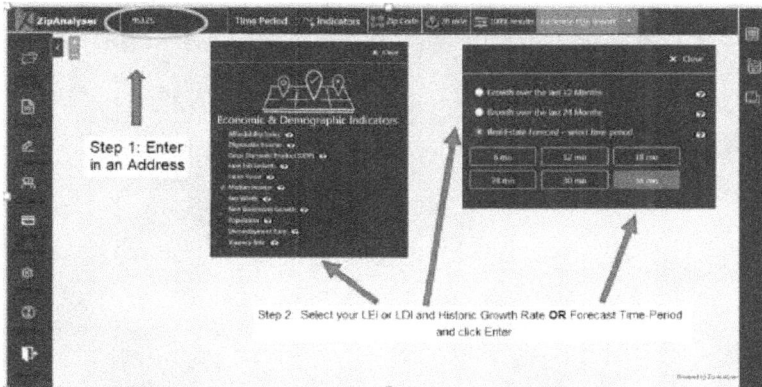

Step 3: In seconds your custom heatmap is generated.

Filter to find top market.

View the latest monthly updated growth

Order your custom report when ready

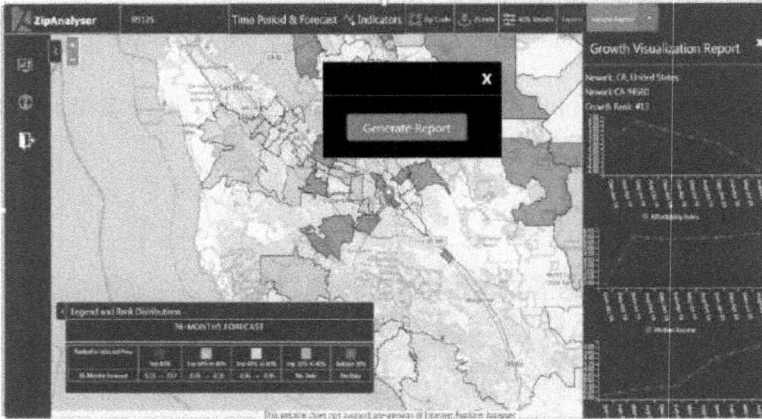

Sample: White Label - Market Intelligence Report

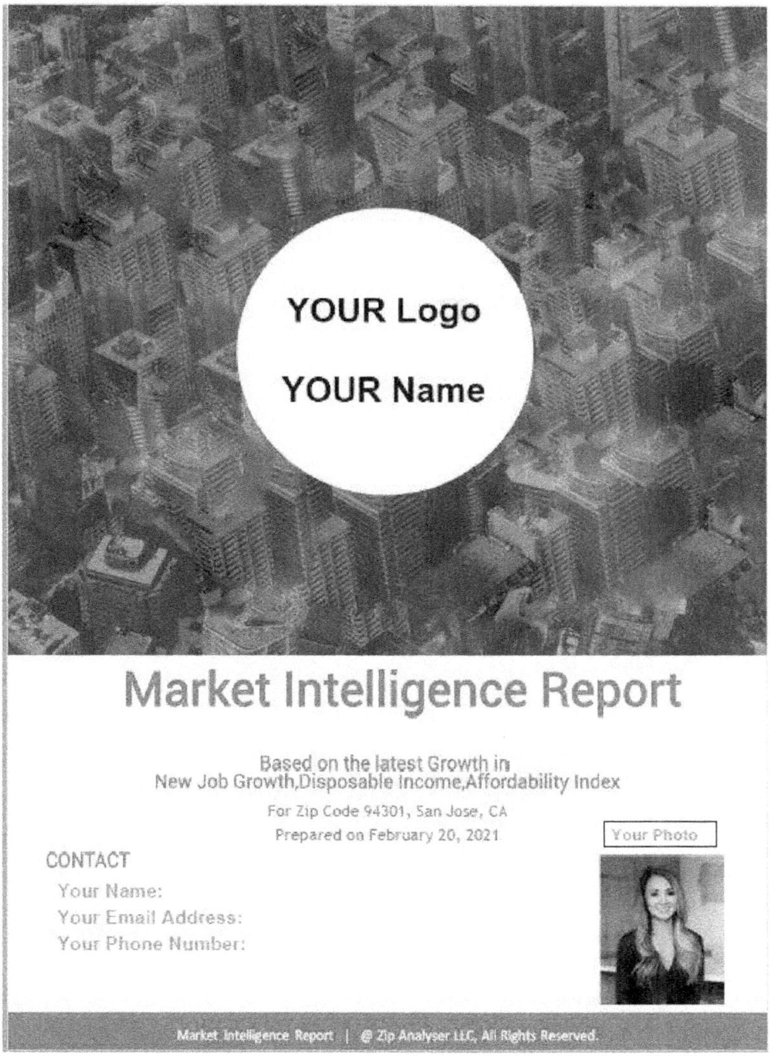

ZipAnalyser

New Job Growth - A Leading Economic Indicator Updated Q1 2021

In the last 24 months, New Job Growth in zip code 94301 has lost -0.11 percent. This compares to a national increase of 0.00 percent.

New Job Growth is defined as assets minus liabilities. It is a concept applicable to individual and a key measure of how much a household is worth. A consistent increase in net worth indicates good financial health.

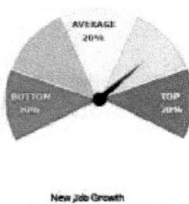

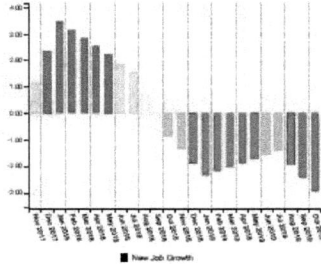

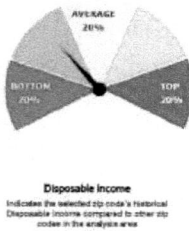

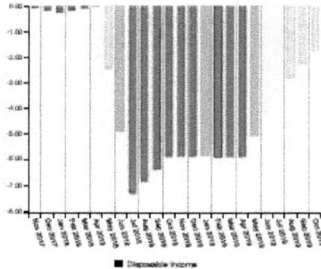

New Job Growth

Indicates the selected zip code's historical New Job Growth compared to other zip codes in the analysis area

New Job Growth

Disposable Income - A Leading Economic Indicator Updated Q1 2021

In the last 24 months, Disposable Income in zip code 94301 has lost -3.73 percent. This compares to a national increase of 0.00 percent.

Disposable Income is defined as assets minus liabilities. It is a concept applicable to individual and a key measure of how much a household is worth. A consistent increase in net worth indicates good financial health.

Disposable Income

Indicates the selected zip code's historical Disposable Income compared to other zip codes in the analysis area

Disposable Income

ZipAnalyser

Affordability Index - A Leading Economic Indicator Updated Q1 2021

In the last 24 months, Affordability Index in zip code 94301 has lost -2.85 percent. This compares to a national increase of 0.00 percent.

Affordability Index is defined as assets minus liabilities. It is a concept applicable to individual and a key measure of how much a household is worth. A consistent increase in net worth indicates good financial health.

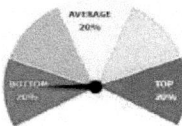

Affordability Index

Indicates the selected zip code's historical Affordability Index compared to other zip codes in the analysis area

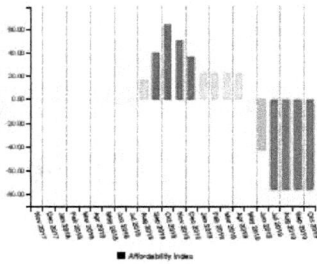

Affordability Index

185

Sample: White Label – Comprehensive Real Estate Forecast Report

YOUR Logo

YOUR Name

Based on **36** Month Real Estate Forecast
and Comprehensive Current Growth Data in San jose, CA

For Zip Code 94301, San Jose, CA
Prepared on February 20, 2021

CONTACT

Your Name:
Your Email Address:
Your Phone Number:

Your Photo

36-Month Real Estate Forecast - Updated Q1 2021

Home values for Zip Code 94301 are forecast to increase by 0.28 percent over the next 24 months. Nationally, prices are forecast to increase by 48087.73 percent.

36-month forecast have an accuracy of ± 2 based upon over 5 years of back testing. With accurate local forecasts, and leading economic indicators, Realtors and investors can limit their risk by assessing the latest growth and forecasts, both locally and regionally.

Type	12-Month Real Estate Forecast	24-Month Real Estate Forecast	36-Month Real Estate Forecast
Zip Code Forecast	0.59	0.28	2.18

187

ZipAnalyser

Affordability Index - A Leading Economic Indicator Updated Q1 2021

In the last 24 months, Affordability Index in Zip Code 94301 has lost -2.86 percent. This compares to a national decrease of -1.34 percent.

Affordability Index is defined as assets minus liabilities. It is a concept applicable to individual and a key measure of how much a household is worth. A consistent increase in net worth indicates good financial health.

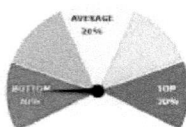

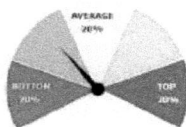

Affordability Index
Indicates the selected Zip Code's historical Affordability Index compared to other Zip Codes in the analysis area

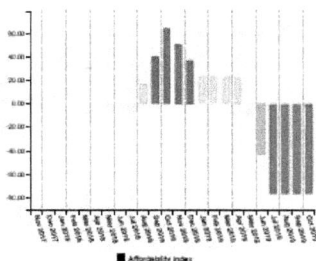

■ Affordability Index

Disposable Income - A Leading Economic Indicator Updated Q1 2021

In the last 24 months, Disposable Income in Zip Code 94301 has lost -5.73 percent. This compares to a national increase of 1.98 percent.

Disposable Income is defined as assets minus liabilities. It is a concept applicable to individual and a key measure of how much a household is worth. A consistent increase in net worth indicates good financial health.

Disposable Income
Indicates the selected zip code's historical Disposable Income compared to other zip codes in the analysis area

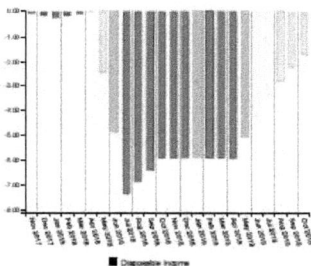

■ Disposable Income

ZipAnalyser

Gross Domestic Product (GDP) - A Leading Economic Indicator Updated Q1 2021

In the last 24 months, Gross Domestic Product (GDP) in Zip Code 94301 has grown 3.33 percent. This compares to a national increase of 5.38 percent.

Gross Domestic Product (GDP) is defined as assets minus liabilities. It is a concept applicable to individual and a key measure of how much a household is worth. A consistent increase in net worth indicates good financial health.

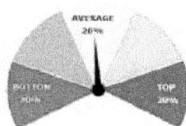

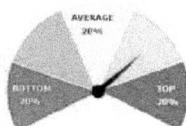

Gross Domestic Product (GDP)
Indicates the selected zip code's historical Gross Domestic Product (GDP) compared to other zip codes in the analysis area

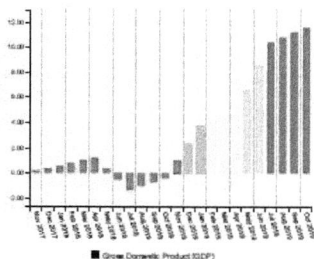

New Job Growth - A Leading Economic Indicator Updated Q1 2021

In the last 24 months, New Job Growth in Zip Code 94301 has lost -0.11 percent. This compares to a national decrease of -0.88 percent.

New Job Growth is defined as assets minus liabilities. It is a concept applicable to individual and a key measure of how much a household is worth. A consistent increase in net worth indicates good financial health.

New Job Growth
Indicates the selected zip code's historical New Job Growth compared to other zip codes in the analysis area

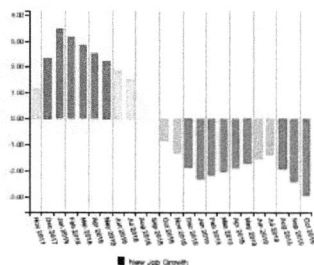

189

ZipAnalyser

Labor Force - A Leading Economic Indicator Updated Q1 2021

In the last 24 months, Labor Force in Zip Code 94301 has grown 6195.35 percent. This compares to a national increase of 29.71 percent.

Labor Force is defined as assets minus liabilities. It is a concept applicable to individual and a key measure of how much a household is worth. A consistent increase in net worth indicates good financial health.

Labor Force
Indicates the selected Zip Code's
historical Labor Force compared to other
Zip Codes in this analysis area

Median Income - A Leading Economic Indicator Updated Q1 2021

In the last 24 months, Median Income in Zip Code 94301 has lost -1.33 percent. This compares to a national increase of 2.10 percent.

Median Income is defined as assets minus liabilities. It is a concept applicable to individual and a key measure of how much is household is worth. A consistent increase in net worth indicates good financial health.

Median Income
Indicates the selected Zip Code's
historical Median Income compared to
other Zip Codes in the analysis area

Sample: CMA or Listing Report with our APIs

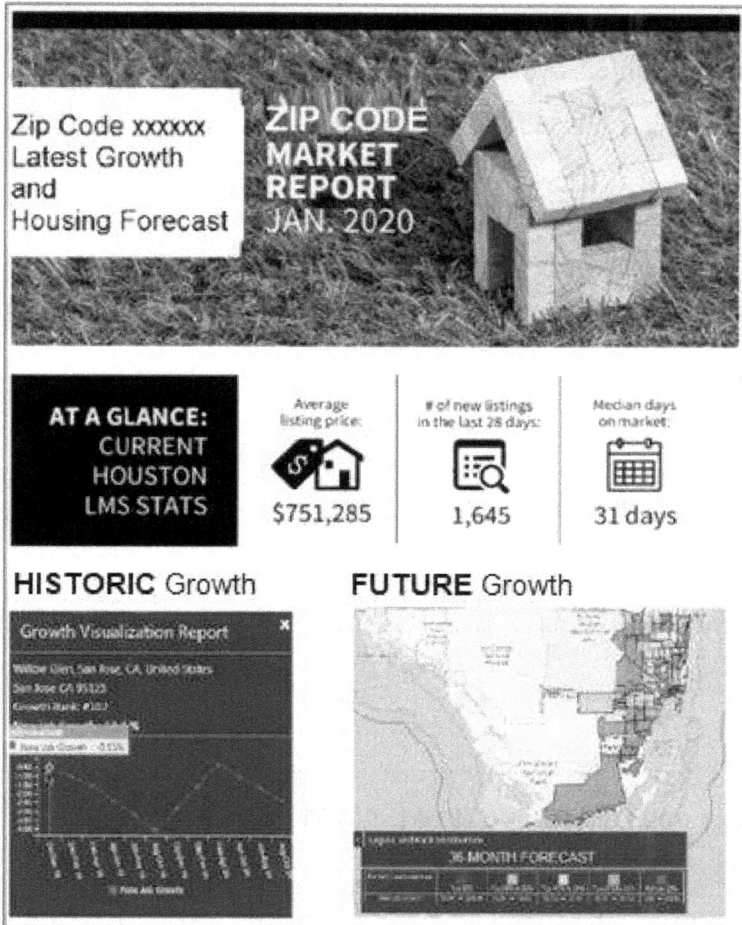

Index

R

S

U

V